STUDIES IN LITERATURE AND STYLE

STUDIES IN LITERATURE AND STYLE

THEODORE W. HUNT

GYAN

Published by

Gyan Publishing House
5, Ansari Road
Daryaganj, New Delhi-110002
Phone: 011-47034999, 9811692060
E-mail: books@gyanbooks.com

Distribution Network
gyanbooks.com
India, USA, Canada, UK, Australia

ISBN: 978-93-7447-481-5 (PB)

First Published, 1906

2nd Impression 2026

Printed at: Gyan Press, Delhi.

STUDIES IN LITERATURE AND STYLE
Author: THEODORE W. HUNT

STUDIES IN LITERATURE AND STYLE.

STUDIES

IN

LITERATURE AND STYLE

BY

THEODORE W. HUNT, PH.D., L.H.D.

Professor of English Philology and Discourse in the College of New Jersey
Editor of Cædmon's "Exodus and Daniel," Author of "Principles of Written Discourse," "English Prose and Prose Writers," etc.

NEW YORK
A. C. ARMSTRONG AND SON
3 & 5 WEST 18th STREET, NEAR 5th AVENUE
1901

PREFACE.

It is the purpose of these Studies to state, discuss and exemplify the representative types of style with primary reference to the needs of the English literary student. As literature is the verbally expressed product of an author's thought and personality, style is the special form given by the writer to such an expression. Back of all formal features in literary art, therefore, there lie intellectual, ethical and personal elements as embodied in the writer. It is one of the leading objects of this volume to study literature and style as thus conditioned. While aiming to present the subject in a method sufficiently logical for purposes of instruction in our literary institutions, we have, also, aimed so to present it as to make it suggestive and helpful to all intelligent readers, and, especially so, to jurists and journalists, and teachers of the truth, in their desire to communicate thought to men in lucid, forcible and attractive forms.

T. W. H.

COLLEGE OF NEW JERSEY,
Princeton, N. J., *Feb.*, *1890.*

TABLE OF CONTENTS.

INTRODUCTORY CHAPTER.

CHAPTER I.

CHAPTER II.

CHAPTER III.

CHAPTER IV.

CHAPTER V.

CHAPTER VI.

CHAPTER VII.

CHAPTER VIII.

CHAPTER IX.

CHAPTER X.

CONCLUDING CHAPTER.

INTRODUCTORY CHAPTER.

THE CLAIMS OF LITERARY STUDIES.

THE generally accepted classification of studies, as now pursued, may be said to be—Science, Philosophy, Art, Language and Literature. It is with the last of these that we have to do in the chapter before us—with Literature, as distinct even from Language. The study of Linguistics, or Philology, is, for our present purpose, one thing; that of Literature, quite another.

By Literary Studies is meant, in a word, the study of authorship in written form, in book and treatise and pamphlet. In the words of Professor Hart, of Ohio, it may be said, quoting in substance, "that literature is the study of life and feeling as it is reflected in the best prose and poetry." Its proper object is, to grasp the author's inner personality and power. In its widest sense, it embraces the expressed written product of all times and peoples—ancient and modern, foreign and native. An examination of the *claims* of such studies to fuller recognition and a more general pursuit is now in place.

I. At the lowest estimate that may be taken of them, they are a source of personal Literary Pleasure. They serve, as Bacon tells us, "for delight," their chief use being, "in privateness and retiring." There is a recreative, refreshing and restful ministry in books, a needed and rational relief from the routine duties of common life. They afford that sense of entertainment to which Maurice refers when he speaks of the Friendship of Books;—to which Lowell refers, in the well-chosen titles of his collections, "Among my Books" and "My Study Windows"; and to which scores of authors, from Bacon to Wordsworth, have gratefully referred. In all periods of life, in youth and early manhood; in later manhood and in old age; in all professions and callings; they come with solace and helpfulness and affectionate counsel.

With what wide variety of topic and treatment, incident and teaching they accost us! In the forms of prose and poetry; biography and history; romance and miscellany; wit and humor and satire; philosophy and morals; maxims and sentiments; social habit and national life—in these and other endless forms, they interest and charm us. Today, in one manner, and, to-morrow, in another; "grave and gay, lively and severe;" suited to our transient moods and fitting in to the changing experiences of life—such studies serve for avocation as well as for vocation, and, as they profit us, also delight and fascinate us.

Perhaps, the main explanation of such a ministry

of pleasure is found in the fact, that the literary studies which we pursue are instinct with the *life* of the minds behind them. The author is in the authorship and gives it a personal potency. We see and hear the man himself conversing with us, and, thus, "choose an author as we choose a friend," on the basis of his individual qualities. That soul must be soured, indeed, and bent on misery for its own sake who cannot, at times, secure surcease of sorrow by communion with the world's gifted spirits who have uttered for us their best thoughts and insist that, despite the anxieties of life, we gratefully receive what they have to offer us of genuine literary pleasure.

II. Such studies present a further and higher claim, in the line of Literary Knowledge. They include what Bacon means when he says, "that reading maketh a full man, so that if a man read little, he need have much cunning to seem to know that he doth not." As a writer in the *Westminster Review* has expressed it, "Books are a means of seeing through other men what we cannot see for ourselves." These literary researches introduce us to the life and times of authors, to that wide area of truth and fact embraced in the broadest scope of such pursuits. They afford us what Mr. Arnold has called, "the criticism of life"; a comprehensive and an ever-widening view of the best thought of the race.

If we take into account but one department of

literary study, we can see at a glance the almost limitless extent of that field of inquiry, observation, reflection and inference to which it conducts us. We refer to what is termed, Literary History, the history of the literature of the most advanced nations. One of the most prominent topics now engaging the attention of our cultivated critics is, the true relation of such a form of history to the origin and progress of literature itself, and the exact value of the historical method in all such studies. Morley and Craik, of England, and Coppee and Tyler, of America, have dwelt largely upon this special feature. In the wider department of general letters, such writers as Hallam, Sismondi, Taine and Possnett, Scherer and Schlegel, have opened to us, in part, the accumulated treasures that lay before them. There is an historico-literary law running through all events and all authorship, binding them together while increasing their separate influence, and no student can examine either aright apart from its relation to the other.

What a spacious and profitable field is opened up in the literature of any one people—say, the French, as we trace it from its beginnings in Celtic Gaul on through the days of the Trouveres and Troubadours to its progressive and culminating expression in the writings of Moliere and Racine! What a vivid picture of early literary development is given us in Arabian letters as far back as the days of the Caliphs, in the eighth century, when every Arabian capital was the centre of authorship and the deadening influence of Mohammedanism alone was able to arrest its rapid growth! What a fund of invaluable knowledge is afforded as we trace the history of Grecian authorship to the Periclean age, or that of Rome to the Augustan, or that of Italy to the days of Petrarch! The full examination of any one period in a classic literature, such as that of Calderon, in Spain, or of Corneille, in France, or of Schiller, in Germany, would be sufficient in itself to repay the diligence of any ingenuous student and inspire him to extend his researches to other countries and periods. Such a survey would embrace all related and tributary topics—ethical and religious, political and social, commercial and practical, educational and æsthetic—in fine, all actual and possible forms of human activity.

So vast has such a province become as it opens up to the advance of the student, and so necessary the narrowing of general discussions to special limits, that the exhaustive knowledge of any one great author is now considered quite sufficient to engage and reward the labors of a lifetime. It is thus that, in Germany, separate chairs have been founded in the universities to interpret the mind and art of Goethe. The same is true of Dante, in the schools of Italy, and of Shakespeare and Milton, in England. Even lesser names than these, as Schiller and Tasso and Pope and Browning, have served to engross the best thought and time of their respective students. The fact that what we now call Shakespeariana, Miltoniana and Coleridgeiana demand separate sections of our libraries to contain them will afford an instance of that rapid multiplication of material that has resulted from an ever more exhaustive study of any one celebrated author.

Such, in part, is the claim of these studies on the score of knowledge secured, so that from the practical point of view, as well as from the pleasurable, such lines of activity must be viewed as most desirable. The well-read man is he who is fully conversant with such a volume of authorship as this; who may be said so to have examined and mastered it, that he has it at his disposal. Such a study is the only basis of accurate and wide-reaching scholarship in letters. Such students feel at home in the libraries of the world, in Athens, in Rome, in Florence and Cordova, in Paris and Weimar, in London and Edinburgh—in the great literary capitals of the ancient and modern world. Whatever else they may or may not know, they feel acquainted with the best minds of the race and with their best mental work as expressed in literary form. Such knowledge is more than mere knowledge. It is a satisfaction and an inspiration, and places us in sympathy with the deepest and purest impulses of the race.

III. We pass to an additional claim in—Literary Culture. More is meant by this than what Bacon includes in his statement—"Studies serve for ornament." Principal Shairp, in his instructive treatise on, "Culture and Religion," calls attention to the three accepted or historical schools of culture—The Ethical, as represented by the Christian church; The Scientific, as represented, especially, by Mr. Huxley, and, The Literary, as best expressed in the person and writings of Mr. Arnold. It is to this third type of culture that we now refer, and, while keeping in view the writings of Mr. Arnold, we shall not feel bound to follow him in all his assertions.

We may note, at the outset, that there is such a thing or product, in a man's personality, as *culture*; distinct, on the one hand, from mere intellect, and, on the other, from merely practical ability. It is difficult, if not impossible, to define it, save by eliminating from it what is not to be confounded with it. It is a something in addition to mere knowledge or learning, though congenial to it and one of its normal results. It is a something in which taste as a faculty and feeling is prominent over every other related power; in which there is ability evinced to discern the presence and quality of the beautiful in nature and art and to enjoy it when discerned. Its effect, wherever fully operative, is to soften and subdue the nature of man. It gives what the artists call *tone* to character. It is synonymous with refinement of spirit and bearing, with that nice regard to the amenities and proprieties which always serves to charm us when it is naturally expressed. More than this, it is a growth, and not a something suddenly secured from without ; the expression of a man's innermost nature and habit, as germane to his being as the light is to the eye or fragrance to the flower.

As to the *forms* it may assume, there are substantially but two.

There is what we designate, General Culture, the normal offspring and evidence of converse with truth in its varied phases and with men of intelligence. Civilization, as we understand the term, is, in part, its cause, and, in part, its effect ; so that we expect to find it modified or conspicuous in proportion to the average or conspicuous place of people in the scale of general enlightenment. In this sense, European culture, as nationally expressed, is in advance of Asiatic. The culture of the Greeks was, thus, superior to that of Rome or any other related people. The Hebrews as a nation lacked it, as do the modern Germans, in comparison with the French. North Europeans, as a class, are inferior, at this point, to South Europeans, and England, by reason of age and environment, is superior to America.

Included in these general influences favorable to general culture there is, in the case of any individual, all that is meant by his educational advantages, the surroundings of home and society and life that so vitally affect him ; companionship with the scholarly and refined ; freedom of access to that great world of natural beauty that lies before every man of common discernment and to that ever-widening world of artistic beauty accessible, in our day, to all who are inclined to avail themselves of it.

We are speaking, however, of Literary Culture, and this, it must be emphasized, is the direct result of *literary* studies as distinct from any other existing form. Scientific studies will not impart it. They tend, in fact, to modify it; if not, indeed, to reduce it to its minimum measure. Philosophical studies, on their intellectual side, will not materially induce it. They are too didactic, technical and speculative to foster its growth. Mere linguistic studies, as an examination of hidden roots and grammatical forms, will not procure it. Even studies in plastic and pictorial art, as a specific branch of intellectual work, will not necessarily induce it. Recognized authorities in science, philosophy, philology and art may be signally devoid of literary taste, as they have been, as a matter of fact, devoid of it. Copernicus and Galileo, as physicists, had nothing of it. Sir Wm. Hamilton, as a psychologist, had but little of it, while the brothers Grimm, in common with most of the great philologists of Germany, make no approach to its possession. The presence of any form of mere mental ability or scholarly acquirement does not secure it. It must be grounded in literary taste, study, habit, and purpose; must be the special product of the study of style in authorship: a study of diction and structure: of qualities and processes: of accuracy of touch on the part of the writer; of his sensibility and finer instincts; of the cast and coloring of his language as distinct from the language itself; of symmetry and fitness of method—in fine, a study in which the artistic and æsthetic have a valid place, us appealing to that sense of beauty supposed to be resident in every rightly constituted mind. It is these Humanities, above all, on which all literary culture is based and without the presence of which we have something short of culture, be it learning, or wisdom or skill.

It is this type of mind and art that Mr. Arnold is ever pressing in his teachings and which may be said to mark, as a law, the literary history of every prominent nation. Lessing, of Germany, was a signal example of artistic taste in letters. Fenelon, of France, was such a writer, while many English authors in the second order of merit, such as Dryden and Pope, Keats and Gray, have evinced its presence in special measure. No literature can be said to be worthy of its name that does not notably possess it. No author can be strictly designated literary who does not substantially express it. No amount of ability or acquisition will altogether atone for its absence, while he is doing an invaluable work for others who insists, as Principal Shairp insists, that all true culture, general or special, finds its best basis in character and contemplates securing the highest ethical ends.

IV. We advance to a final and crowning claim of literary studies in—their Disciplinary Value. We are speaking, it must be noted, of studies, and not merely of reading. It is suggestive to mark, just here, that Lord Bacon's essay on "Reading" is called an essay on Studies, and it is to the disciplinary side of this subject that he refers as he adds —"Studies serve for ability." The position that is here assumed may be sharply contested. It runs directly counter to current opinion, and with many in educated circles would be regarded as a presumption, unwarranted in fact or theory. Literature, as we have been taught to believe, is quite aside from those branches and lines of study that minister to mental breadth and outlook—the incidental pursuit of leisure hours, having no claim to recognition beyond that already expressed, as they contribute to pleasure and culture. The subject, as we view it, is one of immediate interest and value, and may be accorded special discussion at our hands.

The question as to whether literary studies are disciplinary or not in character wholly depends on the view which we hold as to the *scope* and *method* of such studies, and the argument may be safely rested at this point. There are two distinct theories historically held as to literary method. We may call them the Æsthetic and the Intellectual.

The first of these is the current one, under the influence of which most of us have been educated. In this sense, literature means what it has meant in Southern Europe—Polite Letters, or Belles Lettres, and, even here, in the sphere of verse rather than prose. In so far as prose is admissible, it is in its lighter forms; in narrative, descriptive and miscellaneous authorship; in story and sketch and romance. In this sense, it would be questionable to speak of literature as a study or serious pursuit. It takes rank rather as an accomplishment, a convenient and an eminently proper manner of passing one's hours when relieved of specially important duty. Even if allowed a place among studies at all, the order of the study will be that of fact and incident only and the mental result be correspondingly meagre. This is the æsthetic or verbal method, the method hitherto in vogue, on the basis of which it is rightly argued that disciplinary elements, if indeed existing, are reduced to their lowest measure and are, in no sense, potent.

There is, however, a higher and a better method; in fact, the only method consistently before students having a serious purpose in view and having regard to what Bacon would call "the groundwork" of things. We term it the *intellectual* method, the study of literature as an expression of the human mind. It is a study of causes and effects, as seen in authorship; of great laws and principles, stated and applied; of characteristic features, national and personal; of generic and inner forms behind all verbal product; a study of types and tendencies; of helps and hindrances; of race and climate; of place and time and nationality; of the rise and reign and possible decadence of particular schools; of heredity and environment as affecting authorship — in a word, a study of the philosophy of literature and style, as Bascom and Spencer have, respectively, called it; on which conditions, as Mr. Taine insists, all forces and factors must work before any satisfactory conclusions can be reached.

The method before us is, thus, suggestive, comprehensive and logical, as distinct from being technical, narrow and superficial. It is a study of style with primary reference to the thought that is in it. It includes an inquiry into political, social and religious phenomena, and at once co-ordinates literature with every other branch of high learning known to men. It insists upon the detection of a logical nexus in all authorship, national and international, in the light of which all apparent anomalies may be explained, and what Prof. Possnett has called "the world-literature" be seen to move majestically onward, under the benign control of the same great mental laws.

All this, we submit, is in the strictest sense disciplinary; tending directly to the education and enlargement of mental power; entering, at once, as a vital factor into what we call a man's intellectual life. There is, thus, a substantial order of literature, as well as a lighter one, and the substantial is the normal type. There is prose as well as poetry, and prose is the normal type.

There are philosophies and histories and criticisms and discussions, as well as sketches and romances and semi-poetic adventures, and the former are the normal types. As Prof. Garnett has told us—"If reasoning and judgment are faculties of the mind whose training must be kept in view as the objects of literary discipline, where can more suitable means be found to this end than in the study of authors!" "The critical study of literature," adds Dr. Porter, "cannot be overestimated," an order of study, in its disciplinary value, which, according to Pres. Eliot, "has been strangely undervalued."

We are now discussing literary study in its highest phase, as a rational procedure for men of thought in their best moments, as a mental gymnastic among other similar forms of training. How signally this higher view is confirmed, if we pause a moment and examine any separate department of letters! If we speak of history as a literary form, there is a philosophy of history. It is thus that Hallam and Sismondi have written it. How prominent are the higher mental elements of conception, reach and function in the world's great epics, and, more distinctly still, in its dramatic masterpieces! Even in fiction, the most pronounced form of light literature, what a psychological study is offered us in the pages of such authors as Balzac and Victor Hugo; George Eliot and Hawthorne; to say nothing of the intellectual groundwork that lies back of all fiction, as Sidney Lanier, in his "English Novel," has interpreted it!

To apply to such authorship as this the prevailing æsthetic method and call it the only admissible one, or the most desirable one, evinces an utter misconception of literature itself, as, also, a lamentable indifference to the best results it is designed to reach. A sentimental, drawing-room coquetting with literature is one thing; its rational and philosophic pursuit, as the embodiment of the world's best thought to aid us in our thinking, is another, and it is to this latter only that we refer in pressing the claims of such a study upon the attention of the modern student. Pleasure and knowledge and culture and discipline—these, when rightly related and expressed, establish a claim so valid and potent that he who ignores it must justify his attitude and be prepared to tell us just in what particulars and provinces mental discipline is found. Literature is thought in written form. The world's best thinkers are behind it as its explanation, and the world's best interests before it as a motive. Long since, it has entered so vitally and variedly into the mental life of men that no amount of prejudice or erroneous teaching can separate the one from the other, and who of us can tell what he owes of personal power, mentally considered, to those distinctively literary influences that have surrounded him throughout life, and which even now are about us all, as an inspiration and a help!

From this brief discussion, we note two or three suggestions of practical moment, and remark—

1. That such studies should hold a higher place in the *esteem of scholars*. It is a fact patent to all that such esteem has not been heretofore accorded them, nor is such a view at present prevalent. If the course of our reasoning has been correct, and there is a valid benefit in such pursuits, especially in their disciplinary function, then it becomes all men of intelligence to readjust their opinions regarding them. They are to insist that men of letters, if worthy of their calling, belong to the great fraternity of men of learning; that comprehensive scholarship rightly implies an intimate acquaintance with the world's best literature and that the Baconian idea of the rank of authors should be reaffirmed in these modern days.

2. Literary Studies, moreover, should have a larger place in our Liberal Institutions. Accepting it as conceded, that all other leading departments have been accorded their rightful place in our collegiate curricula, it is a fitting time to press anew the claims of the studies now in question. What their position, at present, is, no thoughtful observer of modern education can contemplate without amazement and regret. Despite the fact, that language is taught so prominently in our secondary schools and our colleges, it is lamentable to note how generally it is taught as language only, quite apart from its inner literary quality. It is thus that it comes to pass that students who may have spent the best part of their early life in linguistic study are conspicuously deficient in that phase of

training which is specifically literary. So devoid are they, often, of literary discernment that they may be grammarians, verbal critics, translators, commentators, and accepted authorities in matters of text and structure, and yet be in no true sense, cultured on literary lines—in no true sense, men of letters. We maintain, that language itself cannot be properly taught apart from its innermost literary life ; that whatever place may be assigned to science, philosophy or philology in any course of undergraduate study, a place of equal prominence is to be assigned to studies that are literary. Our institutions of learning should be what they purport to be—literary institutions. Every college should be, as such, an acknowledged literary centre, a home of taste and culture ; an attractive resort for authors, and a school of training from which shall issue, in each successive year, a body of men imbued with literary impulses and determined to advance, in every possible way, the literary interests of the nation. Every college graduate should be a man of letters as of learning, and the influence of all liberal institutions be a controlling one in guiding the literary developments of the people among whom they are established.

3. We emphasize, therefore, the special claims of English Style and English Literary Studies. There is, in every institution of learning, a general literary influence begotten of contact with books and scholars. There is, more specifically still, an influence of a literary character resulting from

classical as distinct from philosophic and scientific studies. We speak, however, of an order of literary pursuit that is purely English—the study of our vernacular authorship and such collateral branches as are necessary to its true interpretation. Such knowledge and culture and training are often lacking where the other forms exist, and serve to show, thereby, the special need of the study of the home literature. Todhunter, Staunton and Thwing have called attention to the subordinate status of such studies in English and American institutions and assert that they form a department second to none in value and interest. There is no conflict here encouraged with any other line of learning; no conflict, certainly, with the study of language, but simply a protest against the scanty space hitherto assigned to English studies in our courses of instruction, and a plea that something like adequate area be given them. If our secondary schools are to do worthier work in this direction, the colleges must invite it and demand it. If teachers of English of high endowment and accurate scholarship are to be at call, when needed, our colleges must train them. If the public literary taste of England and America is to be stronger and purer, or even preserved in its present character, the result is to be reached mainly through the influence of our academic centres. If college and university men are to know, as they ought to know, the literary history, product, spirit and tendencies of the country, the facilities of such knowledge are to be accorded them, so as not to present the anomalous picture of being adepts in every literature save their own. Our vernacular authorship should mainly depend on our colleges for its tone and drift: its scholarly and stable qualities; its purity and moral power over the people. Literary studies of every order must have their rightful place in general esteem and scholarly circles. Not only are we to know the nature of mind and mental, action; the laws of the physical world and the principles of philology; but must further know, and know as fully, how the world's greatest philosophers and scientists and linguists have embodied their thoughts in the best external form; must know the great principles and laws of literary expression; must be able to call the world's great masters in prose and verse our personal friends and helpers, and be able ourselves to utilize all our other knowledge by the ability to embody and express it. Literature, as an essential part of human development and branch of liberal learning, is yet to have its place. The Humanities are, once again, to be reinstated in their old position of prominence. The gross, material tendencies of the day, so dominant and exacting, must speedily yield to better influences. The book and the pen are, yet again, to shape events. The library is yet to rule the world.

CHAPTER I.

THE INTELLECTUAL STYLE.

STYLE may be said to be as diversified as human personality. If, as Buffon tells us, "the style is the man," then the method or manner in which thought may be embodied and verbally expressed may be as varied as are the multiform phases of what we call humanity, or human nature.

Some of these *bases* or principles of classification may here be mentioned.

We may speak of style as conditioned by *racial* peculiarities. Hence, the North European, as illustrated in the German; the South European, as in the French and Italian. We speak of the classical style of the older empires, as distinct from that of the modern European nations. Literary historians tell us of the Asiatic style; that exuberant, pictorial and florid manner so germane to the Oriental nations, as distinct from the Occidental and more practical peoples. There is a style peculiar to England, as it differs in its national type from America. In the British Isles themselves, the Scotch, the Irish and the English evince unique phases of expression, growing out of civic and local differences. Mr. Arnold, in his critical writings, is never weary of calling our attention to what he terms the Hellenic style, as distinct from the Hebraic or Palestinean; meaning, by the one, the highly artistic order of the Greek, and, by the other, a more solid and serious type, Judaic in its character.

If, as a further principle, we look at style from the view-point of *age* or *period*, we may speak of the ancient, mediæval and modern styles; of the style of the Renaissance in Italy; of that of the era of Louis XIV. in France; and that of the Elizabethan, Augustan, Georgian and Victorian ages, in England.

Emphasizing the *names* of prominent authors as exponents of separate orders of style, we rightly speak of the Platonic and Ciceronian and Socratic styles; of the Lutheran and Pascalian; of the Baconian, Addisonian and Websterian.

Studying style in the light of *structure*, *motive* and *spirit*, we speak, still further, of the critical and the romantic styles; of the realistic and the imaginative; of the direct and antithetic; of the simple and metaphysical; of the idiomatic and foreign; of style conditioned by personal temperament, as the mercurial and phlegmatic; of style as lucid, concise, finished, forensic, oratorical, disputative, expository, philosophic and ornate. In fine, style, as suggested, is as varied as the character, ability, experience, engagements and objects of men; the manifestation of soul and mind and life in all their possible forms.

There are, however, some types and orders of style that may be said to be standard, fundamental and all-inclusive, and which, as such, deserve a separate discussion at our hands. We shall call them the Intellectual, the Literary, the Impassioned and the Popular; including, respectively, such additional forms as—the Critical, the Poetic, the Satirical and the Humorous. They may be said to represent, respectively, intelligence, taste, feeling and pleasure. Each will be seen to have its own well-defined area and object, while they together make up the sum-total of what is called style, in literary art.

THE INTELLECTUAL STYLE.

Prof. Bain, in a recent treatise on discourse, dwells at length on the Intellectual Elements of Style. Prof. Bascom, of our own country, has written an able volume on the "Philosophy of Style," following the line of discussion opened up for him by Herbert Spencer, of England. Such writers as Schlegel, in his "Philosophy of Language;" Campbell, in his "Philosophy of Rhetoric," and Lord Kames, in his treatise on Criticism, have represented and developed this intellectual feature of style.

The very definition of discourse, with which we must begin all discussion, would seem to demand the admission of this view. We define it as the expression of thought, the outer form in which ideas are presented. Apart from the presence and prominence of such inherent ideas, behind all outer presentation, there is no occasion for expression. To write, Max Müller would say, is "to think verbally." He would call expression, the "science of thought," applied as an art; a thinking with pen in hand, as we contemplate the oral utterance of our ideas. There is a true sense, therefore, in which it may be said that the words—style and intellect—are mutually inclusive and explanatory, so that, in every worthy act of expression, they must go together. It was this exalted view of the nature and function of style that De Quincey so strongly held and so ably exemplified. It is thus that his writings, miscellaneous as they are, are freighted with meaning and to him who carefully reads them must minister mental strength and richness.

We are now prepared to state and explain the two or three cardinal *characteristics* of the style before us.

I. Emphasis of Subject Matter over Form. The great question with the intellectual writer is, How can the truth be made intelligible? How can the minds of readers be most effectually reached and the importance of what is written be seen for its own intrinsic merit, rather than because presented by this or that author, in this or that manner?

Such a writer feels, first of all, that he must have

a clear and full perception of the truth to be communicated; must be profoundly convinced of the fact that it is the truth, and be inflamed with a fervent desire to make it known for the well-being of others. Such a style is based on the essential value of the truth as independent of any worth that may lie in the special exposition of it and is never so well satisfied as when the writer is lost in the writing.

Historical style, when expressed in its highest forms, is essentially intellectual. Its basis is truth. Its object is instruction. Its methods are logical and rational, and its pervading spirit, love of the truth for the truth's sake and for what it may accomplish on behalf of others. Mr. Grote's "History of Greece;" Thomas Warton's "History of English Poetry;" Froude's "History of England;" Schlegel's "History of Philosophy;" Hallam's "History of Literature" and Shedd's "History of Christian Doctrine" are such histories, affording conspicuous examples of style as intellectual. If we compare such treatises with Macaulay's "History of England;" McCarthy's "History of Our Own Times" and McMaster's "History of the People of the United States," we see, at once, the striking difference in favor of the former on the ground of their superior intellectuality. They are more than simple narratives—a pleasing and facile recital of events. They make us think as we read them. They stir within us the best judgment that we have and lead us on from sequence to sequence through a series of connected causes to some final and all-embracing result.

Within the domain of history, and outside of it, it would not be amiss to call such a style, *philosophical.* Hooker, in his "Ecclesiastical Polity;" Bacon, in his "Advancement of Learning;" Addison, in his criticism of "Paradise Lost;" Clarendon, in his "Discourses on Government;" Dryden, in his "Critical Prefaces;" Adam Smith, in his "Wealth of Nations;" Blackstone, in his "Commentaries;" Cudworth, in his "Intellectual System of the Universe;" Hobbes, in his "Leviathan;" Whewell, in his "Inductive Sciences" and Coleridge, in his Shakespearean discussions, have written intellectually in the sense that they have written profoundly and philosophically. Such writings are marked by the persistent prominence of the subject matter, and, hence, are marked by such qualities as weight, condensation, thoroughness, mental insight and equipoise.

It is wholly logical, therefore, to speak of a solid style—a style with body or substance. This eliminated, style is reduced to an idle collocation of words for the words' sake, and passes, at once, from the high plane of a mental gymnastic to that of a mere verbal entertainment, belittling alike to author and reader.

II. We note an additional feature of the style before us—Comprehensiveness of View.

There must be not only depth and clearness of

insight, but breadth of outlook, a wide and an ever-widening extension of the boundary of knowledge. In the procedure and final purpose of the intellectual writer, there is no place for restriction. The field is the world and nothing less than an all-embracing view of the related unity of truth must satisfy him. Where others hesitate, he must advance. Where inferior writers are narrow in their speculations and conclusions, he must be unlimited and catholic. The intellectual style is notable for its range and reach. Occupying higher ground than is ordinarily assumed, it has, presumably, a more spacious field of observation, and is at fault if it does not see farther than others on lower levels.

Some undoubted examples of this mental many-sidedness may be cited. Guizot and Buckle, in their respective discussions of "European Civilization;" Principal Shairp, in his treatment of "English Poetry;" Professor Masson, in his "Life and Times of Milton;" Mr. Bancroft, in his "History of the United States;" Mr. Lecky, in his "History of England in the Eighteenth Century," and "History of European Morals," are such authors. In these books, and such as these, the reader is at once impressed with their intellectual area, with the ground that they cover; not in the superficial sense of mere extension, but in the philosophic sense of comprehensiveness of view. They leave nothing that is valuable unnoticed. In a true sense, they exhaust the subject, in so far as any knowledge of it is, at present, possible.

It is for this reason, as much as for any other, that such books, presenting such a style, are the books that still live and will live, either in their separate personality, as books, or in the practical use which all succeeding authors make of them. Bacon's "Novum Organum;" Aristotle's "Poetics and Politics;" Fenelon's "Dialogues on Eloquence;" Schlegel's "Dramatic Literature;" Warburton's "Divine Legation;" Mills' "Representative Government" and Longinus' treatise "On the Sublime" are works that do not die or serve their purpose with the times that produced them. They are, rather, for all time, and reappear, in varied forms, in the writings of succeeding authors discussing similar subjects. In their wide range of view, they have, once for all, taken the observations needed, and nothing can nullify their results, save that gradual enlargement of the province of knowledge which of necessity results from the general progress of the race. It is mainly by reason of this mental comprehensiveness that such a style is stimulating and inspiring. There is everything in it to quicken mental endeavor and prompt the soul to its best efforts in conception and execution. Originality in authorship is found here, if anywhere, while, quite apart from pure creation or invention, there is that discovery of truth, hitherto unseen, which, to all intents and purposes, has the value of original truth itself.

It is for this reason, among others, that the style of Carlyle and of Emerson is so potent in its influence. With all their faults of form and process, they are intellectual authors in the sense of being far-sighted and original. No man in England wrote as Carlyle did, and no one in America, just as Emerson did. They are more than eccentric and unique. They are original, from beginning to end. Looking over the same ground as do others, they look with their own eyes and genius. The opinion stoutly maintained by some critics, that Mr. Emerson has influenced American thought more profoundly than any other American author has done, finds much of its basis in this quality of style of which we are now speaking—that original comprehensiveness of view that saw the truth in its entirety and expressed it in a form purely Emersonian, and, therefore, intellectual.

III. Sobriety of Spirit. This is one of the manifest marks of any writer of sterling merit or any style of permanent influence. The relation of the writer and the style to the truth is, of itself, sufficient to make them sedate. It is to this type of authorship that Mr. Arnold refers in the suggestive phrase—"intellectual seriousness," by which he means, a sense of responsibility, becoming any one whose mission in the world is the discovery and circulation of the truth. It is what Longinus would call "elevation of spirit and sentiment," that Ciceronian order of expression that is always devout and deferential; dealing with high themes in an exalted manner, immeasurably above all that is trivial and common.

Such a feature of style is ethical as much as it is intellectual. It is, indeed, the ethical side of mental activity as expressed in the work of the writer. As he writes, it evinces itself in various forms—in an impartial accuracy of statement and opinion; in a kind of judicial gravity of mind that will ensure honest results in the face of temptations to the contrary: in the avoidance of every circuitous and questionable method; in the supremacy of judgment over passion; of conscience over personal preference, and in a loyal devotion to the interests of truth.

We have spoken of Mr. Emerson, in other connections. His style may be here adduced as second to that of no other author in its sobriety of character and aim. His style, as his philosophy, was transcendental; always expanding in that upper air of moral purity that makes his writings ethically healthful to all who read and understand them. Thomas Arnold, of Rugby, was conspicuous for this particular feature. It was because he was the man that he was, that the method of his utterance was always marked by a kind of senatorial sedateness. John Milton, in his English prose, as in his verse, evinced this quality in a pronounced degree. The possession of a good degree of it by Edmund Burke has given to his forensic efforts a notable place in English Letters, while the writings of some of his more gifted contemporaries became obsolete with the occasions that evoked them. The late Mr. Whipple, of our own country, signally illustrated this excellence. He was always in sober earnest as a writer. Whether he treats of Elizabethan or American Literature, the reader will never be disappointed in finding an author who carries his conscience with him where-ever he goes. In his suggestive papers on "Eminent Men," such as Agassiz and Webster, he is perfectly at home and at his best, in that he could bring to their discussion the fullest measure of his mental sobriety. Thomas Carlyle, despite his errors of character and style, will always have a commanding place in our literary history, if for no other reason than for this, that he never approached a theme or conducted its discussion without a kind of personal reverence of manner; that Teutonic gravity of bearing and address which served, on the one hand, to secure a dispassionate treatment of the subject, and, also, on the other, to enlist the deepest ethical sympathies of the reader.

If we compare the Germans with the French, at this point, we find them to differ as to the presence or absence, respectively, of this ethical feature in mental and literary work. Teutonic style, in all its natural types, is intellectually devout; marked by that Gothic or Germanic seriousness which is one of the prime features of the North of Europe. Göethe and Schiller, Lessing and Herder, Klopstock and Wieland were writers of this order, while a light and often flippant spirit marks much of the authorship of Southern Europe.

Such, among others, are the three most essential features of the style Intellectual, and they must exist in some good degree of manifestation. It is their presence which more than all else may be said to give character to style, making it a potential element in the world's mental progress. Authorship, after all, must be ranked in the light of its intellectual qualities, back of all that is merely verbal or æsthetic. The ancients were right in making the study of style a part of philosophy itself, an integral chapter in the study of mind.

METHODS OF CULTIVATION.

As to any particular method by which such an order of style may be cultivated, it may be affirmed, that, in a true sense, it is independent of all method, being largely, if not mainly, due to the writer's antecedents and personality. Where an author's early training has been a thorough one; where all of his early associations have been healthful; where, above all, his own habit of mind has been reflective and logical; where, in a word, his individuality has been and is intellectual, his style must be of the same superior order. He must speak and write as he thinks and because he thinks. All that he utters or records will, necessarily, be marked by a mental tone and cast. It is very rarely, in the history of authorship, that a writer, so happily situated and endowed, becomes a superficial writer or even degenerates into the adoption of any one of the inferior forms of literary work.

There is such a thing as an inherited bias toward the rational and profound. There is such a thing as a genius for the substantial and the meditative; a constitutional love for the truth in its deepest and purest forms. Lord Brougham, of England, in his parliamentary and judicial efforts was, from the first, such an author. Mr. Gladstone, when at Eton, was a thoughtful English boy, and when at Oxford, long before he rose to distinction as a writer and a statesman, impressed all about him with the mental gravity of his speech and bearing. John Quincy Adams was a man of this exalted type. "He spoke and wrote with a manly sobriety," says his latest biographer, "because of the manliness of character that was in him." Alexander Hamilton was such a writer, within the sphere of American constitutional law; as was Rufus Choate, on civil and criminal jurisprudence. In the province of English Fiction, George Eliot is a distinctively intellectual writer, mainly because of the innate quality of her mind and tastes, and so on throughout the list of the world's most philosophic authors.

If, however, the question of method is pressed to an answer, we would say—that this special type of style is best secured by keeping in active connection with *mental life and work.* Mr. Hamerton has written a book on, "The Intellectual Life."

It is with such a life that the ambitious author must keep himself in sympathy. He must keep every mental faculty within him in constant exercise, up to the full limit of its possible activity. His judgment, reason, perception and general mental life must be under daily discipline. Every temptation to personal indolence ; to the abuse, misuse or neglect of his natural endowments must be resisted. As the old writers would have expressed it, he must keep his wits or *intellectuals* about him so as to make them capable of increasingly superior work. It is this very necessity that makes the style before us so desirable—in that it demands intellectual activity in all departments open to the writer. It is a style connected with all the highest mental aims ; in which all our best acquisitions and training can be utilized, and which becomes, thereby, an integral factor in our personal progress and usefulness.

There is an imminent danger, just here, it is true, in the direction of a style unduly intellectual, so that it becomes technical, unpractical and unfeeling—the professional utterance of the author rather than a free and sympathetic expression of views. Intellectuality tends to the abstract and speculative. It tends, when unguarded, to widen the distance between author and reader, and thus to defeat the ultimate purpose of all expression.

This temptation or tendency may, however, be overcome. A writer may be, in the best sense, scholarly without being, in the objectionable sense, scholastic. He may be abstract without being abstruse: a prose writer, without being prosaic; a man, as well as an author. The writer, as a thinker, must keep himself in sympathy with human life; must be a man of the world as well as of books; must appreciate the relations that connect his study with the street and when he writes, be it never so professionally, write so as to be intelligible to readers less profound than he. It is a part of his duty as an intellectual writer to make plain what is difficult; to present hidden truth in open form and to lift his readers to higher mental levels.

We simply insist, that the writer must be a thinker; that he should express his thought, primarily, for the sake of the thought, and not of the form, so that any one perusing his pages shall feel the impulses of mental quickening and rise from the reading stronger in mental fibre and calibre than before.

We note, by way of suggestion, that the intellectual style in authorship is needed in aii periods of a nation's literary history to counteract the inevitable tendency to the *inferior* and *superficial.* Such a tendency is especially prominent in our age and nation. It is the age of poetry, in its lighter forms; and of prose, in the forms of fiction, and descriptive miscellany. In and of themselves, there is nothing objectionable in these forms, if, indeed, they do not become the exclusive or dominant types. That they may not become so, certain counteracting agencies are needed—those weightier and more substantial orders of prose expression that serve to steady literature and give it permanence in history. This is one of the primary offices of the style before us. It opposes the undue influences of the unintellectual in writing. It insists upon the primacy of mental faculty and method in letters over all else that may compete with it. It holds that the author shall, first of all, be the thinker.

Hence, prose must be prominent over poetry; historical and philosophic prose over the descriptive, miscellaneous and imaginative; the mental and ethical, over the æsthetic. In our time and nation, when books are fast giving way to pamphlets, periodicals and the daily issues of the press; when public taste is satisfied with an order of literature designed, only, to divert the attention for the moment; it is solemnly incumbent on the educated writer to bring the educational elements of style to the front; to raise the standard of common criticism in questions of authorship, and to write, as Milton wrote, for the "times succeeding." An author, by the very etymology of the word, is one who adds to the sum of human knowledge; who, in the true Baconian sense, aims by his pen to secure the advancement of learning.

The Intellectual style, we may add, is, by way of emphasis, the style of the *student* and the *scholar*, specially adapted to his introspective habit and to the general tenor of his daily work as a seeker after truth. University and college men should, as such, be personally partial to its acquisition and practice; should view it and defend it as the first order of style, and insist, both in their undergraduate and graduate life, that, when they write, they write in a scholarly manner, not properly expected of those outside the pale of educational privilege. In the present dangerous drift of English style toward the superficial and flippant, what is to become, we submit, of general literary taste and the best interests of our national authorship, if English and American students fail to apply the discipline they have received and are receiving to the definite province of literary work, in the form of a stable, thoughtful, Websterian style? Next to God himself, the greatest entity in the world is, Thought—the greatest force among forces, the greatest factor in the progress of the race: and when a man sits down to write, in the self-assumed character of a teacher of men, the rational presumption is, that he has something to say for which the world has been waiting; by which the existing product of human intelligence shall be increased or revived. Style, we repeat, postulates thought and a thinker, and, in justice to this its fundamental postulate and its final purpose, must be, in the truest sense of the term, intellectual.

INTELLECTUAL STYLE.

Examples.

Another error, of a diverse nature from all the former, is the over-early and peremptory reduction of knowledge into arts and methods; from which time, commonly, sciences receive small or no augmentation. But as young men, when they knit and shape perfectly, do seldom grow to a further stature, so knowledge, while it is in aphorisms and observations, it is in growth, but when it once is comprehended in exact methods, it may perchance be further polished and accommodated for use and practice; but it increaseth no more in substance. Another error is an impatience of doubt and haste to assertion, without due and mature suspension of judgment. For the two ways of contemplation are not unlike the two ways of action, commonly spoken of by the ancients; the one, plain and smooth, in the beginning and in the end, impassable; the other, rough and troublesome, in the entrance, but, after a while, fair and even; so it is in contemplation; if a man will begin with certainties, he shall end in doubts; but if he will be content to begin with doubts, he shall end in certainties.

But the greatest error of all the rest is, the mistaking or misplacing of the last or furthest end of knowledge. For men have entered into a desire of learning and knowledge, sometimes, upon a natural curiosity, and inquisitive appetite; sometimes, to entertain their minds with variety and delight; sometimes, for ornament and reputation; and, sometimes, to enable them to victory of wit and contradiction; and, most times, for lucre and profession, and, seldom, sincerely to give a true account of their gift of reason to the benefit and use of men.—*Bacon's "Advancement of Learning."*

In that great social organ, which, collectively, we call Literature, there may be distinguished two separate offices that may blend, and often do so, but capable, severally, of a severe insulation, and naturally fitted for reciprocal repulsion. There is, first, the literature of knowledge, and, secondly, the literature of power. The function of the first is to teach; the function of the second is to move. The first speaks to the mere discursive understanding; the second speaks, ultimately, it may happen, to the higher understanding or reason, but always through affections of pleasure and sympathy. . . . It is in relation to these great moral capacities of man that the literature of power lies and has its field of action. It is concerned with what is highest in man; for the Scriptures themselves never condescend to deal, by suggestion or co-operation, with the mere discursive understanding. The very highest work that has ever existed in the literature of knowledge is but a provisional work, a book upon trial and sufferance. Whereas, the feeblest works in the literature of power, surviving at all, survive as finished and unalterable amongst men.—*De Quincey's "Miscellanies."*

Extension, we know, is a very imperfect measure of things; and the length of the sun's journeying can no more tell us how far life has advanced than the acreage of a field can tell us what growths may be active within it. A man may go south and stumbling over a bone, may meditate upon it till he has found a new starting point for anatomy; or eastward and discover a new key to language, telling a new story of races; or he may head a new expedition that opens new continental pathways, get himself maimed in body, and go through a whole heroic poem of resolve and endurance and, at the end of a few months, he may come back to find his neighbors grumbling at the same parish grievance as before. . . . If the simplest thinking has about the force of a greyhound, the slowest must be suffered to move, like the limpet, by an apparent sticking, which after a good while is discerned to be a slight progression. Such differences are manifest in the variable intensity which we call human experience, from a revolutionary rush of change which makes a new inner and outer life to that quiet recurrence of the familiar which has no other epochs than those of hunger and the heavens.—*George Eliot's "Daniel Deronda."*

I would here observe that the question concerning the origin of Christianity cannot be disposed of by a general reference to the facility with which mankind are deluded and the frequency of impostures in the world. To put aside the question of its origin by telling us that mankind are easily deceived, is much the same as it would be to put aside the question about the origin of the Gulf Stream by telling us that water is an element very easily moved in different directions. The origin of such a movement is to be investigated. To me, when I look at this religion commending itself to the conscience of men ; meeting all his moral wants and embosoming the only true principles of economical and political science, it no more seems possible that the system of Christianity should have been originated or sustained by man than it does that the ocean should have been made by him.—*Mark Hopkins' "Lowell Lectures."*

CHAPTER II.

THE LITERARY STYLE.

THIS is an order of style that lies midway between the Intellectual and the Popular; bordering more closely, however, upon the former than upon the latter. It is that order of style which seems to be united, according to the current and correct view, with literature itself—the style of authors and of books, the style of the library and the man of letters; removed, as far as possible, from the scientific, technical and speculative, as it is, also, from the ordinary and commonplace. Based on literature itself as a distinctive branch of human activity, it may be supposed to progress and decline in obedience to the rise or retrogression of literary art and taste.

In what are called, the Golden Ages of Letters—as the Periclean age, of Greece; the Augustan age, of Rome; the age of Louis XIV., in France and that of Elizabeth, in England, it would naturally have reached as it did, the climax of its excellence; as it reached, also, the lowest level of its decadence in such eras of English decline as that of the century and a half between Chaucer and Spencer or that of the Restoration of Charles II. Every civilized and advancing people may be presumed, at one period or another in its history, specially to exhibit it, even though, as in Spain, Portugal, Italy and other European nations, literary historians are obliged to refer to it as an order of style far back in the heroic and traditional past. An examination of some of its salient features will reveal its essential nature and objects.

I. Ease and Naturalness of Expression. This is one of the first and strongest impressions made upon the mind by a master of the Literary style. There is, everywhere, the evidence of fluency and facility of touch—the impression made that the writer has a vocabulary at his disposal more than sufficient for all the demands that he may have to make upon it, in the course of his writing.

Nor is such a readiness or expression confined to the mere diction or phraseology of the author, but lies far below the word itself, within the very nature of the subject matter. There is an inner freedom of mental movement, as well as an outer freedom of word and structure. The thought itself is flexible and pliant, easily adapting itself to the ever-changing temperament of the author and reader. The old critics were wont to call it, the flowing style, moving along on its unfettered way, from point to point of its progress, as quietly and smoothly as a silvery stream through an English meadow. So natural and free is the movement, that it gives to the reader the impression of absolute artlessness. Everything seems spontaneous and unstudied; so decidedly facile as to seem to have required no reflection whatever on the part of the author, in order to its final expression. Nature and art are made so congenial and are so conjoined in the unified method, that all specific processes of plan and discussion are successfully concealed, and the reader is never allowed to enter, even approximately, into the interior literary habit of the author.

What is, sometimes, called versatility, in style, is alike a cause and an effect of such an unrestrained deliverance of thought. An almost limitless variety marks the page. No two topics are approached and developed in the same manner. Even the same topic is presented from all possible points of view, so that the principle of diversity itself will secure to the style the impression of flexibility and ease.

One of the special charms of the "Essays of Elia," of the "Noctes Ambrosianæ" and of Addison's "Spectator" is found in this consummate naturalness of movement. There is nothing rigid, conventional or scholastic; nothing to remind one that as the authors were producing their work, they were thinking at all of the manner of producing it. On the contrary, so life-like is the presentation, that the successive papers become colloquial in their character, a kind of face to face conversation, in the most informal manner, on the current questions of politics, society and taste. Mr. Prescott, the American historian, is notable for this racy and unaffected style, as are, also, Knight and Green, of England. In the department of fiction, It is conspicuous in Dickens, De Foe, Kingsley and Sir Walter Scott. In ethical allegory, Bunyan is unsurpassed in its illustration, while, in the spacious province of general descriptive prose, such writers as Goldsmith, Steele, Sidney Smith, Horace Walpole, Thomas Hughes, the Brothers Hare and the French philosopher, Descartes, are so justly distinguished for this verbal and mental opulence, as to make us feel, as we read them, that it is as easy a matter for them to write as they do, as it is for a bird to sing, a flower to bloom, or a sensitive maiden to blush.

II. We notice an additional feature of the literary style in—Its Dignity of Manner, corresponding, somewhat, to sobriety of spirit, in the style Intellectual. Longinus, the Greek critic, would call it, elevation of spirit. It is germane, in its character, to what appears in epic poetry under the name of sublimity—a kind of lofty bearing of soul which the writer naturally assumes, as he contemplates the treatment of high and majestic themes. There is, beyond question, in all purely literary work, a subdued and scholarly composure; partly, the product of the author's personality; and, largely, the product of the particular kind of work in which as a writer he is spending his life and energy.

The man of letters, by the very character of his calling, is, in the true sense, a recluse, necessarily separated from the common pursuits and ambitions of his fellows. He is not, on the one hand, a strictly professional man, nor yet a man of business and affairs, but one who occupies a place and rank of his own, with its own engagements, objects and rewards. It is his, as it is no other's, to hold constant converse with the Muses; to keep himself in mental and spiritual preparation for such exalted fellowship. In this sense, the author is unworldly in his associations and employments, having but little to do with that "mundane" school of letters to which Mr. Gosse is of late so fond of referring. His sphere of residence and effort is somewhat above the plane of common life and it is eminently fitting that he evince a corresponding dignity of demeanor. Such a writer will repel, as unworthy of him, all that is base and belittling, and will aim, at every stage, to magnify his office by a kind of courteous and scholarly reserve.

It is not to be forgotten, indeed, that there is a danger, just here, to which not a few exponents of Literary style have partially yielded, in that this reserve has over-reached itself and taken the form of a decided *isolation* from the every-day life of men—a haughty bearing among their fellows, quite out of keeping with their avowed mission as teachers of the truth to men. Literary writers, as a class, are far too apt to be clannish and unsympathetic in their natural desire to keep " far from the madding crowd," scorning perhaps, with an unfortunate pride, that very constituency on whose patronage they depend for appreciation and support. Such an unseemly spirit is often the result of advancing years, as with Carlyle and Tennyson ; this selfish and cynical tendency growing with the debility and disappointments of age, and we wonder whether the almost caustic couplets of the second "Locksley Hall" are the actual product of the genial author of the first "Locksley Hall," of "Enoch Arden" and " Lady Godiva." Gibbon evinced something of this unliterary crabbedness, as did Pope, Hume, Hobbes, Doctor Johnson, Gifford and Jeffrey, Byron and Swift, Charles Reade and the Earl of Beaconsfield ; while it may be said to be a characteristic feature of those literary charlatans and amateurs of every age who atone for the absence of genuine merit by a self-assumed superiority over what they are pleased to call, the common authors of the day.

Such a spirit, however, is no part of the truly literary style, but its open violation and abuse,—an extreme application of a principle creditable in itself—that of a noble and scholarly retiracy of manner as opposed to all that is presumptuous and puerile. Walter Savage Landor, as a poet and prose writer, is an illustrious example of this elevated and urbane order of style. No finer specimens of dignity in letters can be seen than that evinced in the pages of this author's "Imaginary Conversations," in which, as he represents the greatest authors of all history holding high converse on exalted themes, he himself is in fullest sympathy with the theme and adds dignity to dignity by the personal decorum of his manner. The English essayist, John Foster, is of this order of writers, as are De Quincey, Doctor Arnold, Cardinal Newman and Sir James Mackintosh, in the same department of authorship. The great William Pitt, in his forensic style, illustrates this same magisterial bearing, while, in the two special departments of philosophical and pulpit prose, English is conspicuously rich in such names as—Chillingworth, Cudworth, Maurice and Chalmers. Hugh Miller, of England, as a literary scientist exhibited it, as did Hannah More among English authoresses. What a unique example of this classical dignity was our American poet, Longfellow, equally at home with the *savans* and the children who thronged about him and never, in one instance, condescending, in any unworthy way, to compromise his high vocation as an author! Edward Everett, in his best literary work, was second to no eminent author of his day in the quiet majesty of his presence and address, so that all who came within the circle of his influence were chastened and uplifted. Whatever merits these authors possessed, they lived and wrote on the loftiest levels, and have given English and American literature a status in history from which it would be difficult to remove it. Their presence and their productions alike rebuke all that is undignified in letters and go far to counteract all tendencies to the unseemly.

III. We note a further and most significant element of the style before us, in its Artistic Finish. Emphasizing what has been said, in other connections, as to the vital relations of external form to inner thought, it is still perfectly consistent to say, that there is such a feature of all true style as grace or beauty of form ; an outward attractiveness of appearance, different in character from anything belonging to the subject matter itself.

Style, or the art of expression, is a fine art as well as a useful art, designed to be conducive to all the highest kinds of literary pleasure. Though its main purpose is secured in the direction of mental quickening, it has an additional and a valuable purpose in the line of ministering to that sense of the elegant and refined which is inherent in the soul and must be satisfied. Verbal expression has an æsthetic quality and aim. Unity and Symmetry in writing are not only logical features, demanding the proper adjustment of part to part, but are, as well, artistic or architectural features, without the valid presence of which no amount of mere mental ability will fully suffice. What we call, proportion, is as attractive in a poem or prose production as in a building or a painting.

In a word, the element of correct and disciplined

taste enters as an integral factor into all good style and, where it is especially prominent, makes the style literary rather than intellectual. Mr. Ruskin's style is eminently literary, as an æsthetic discussion of æsthetic topics, whereby the principles and laws of the beautiful are set forth in a manner satisfactory to the demands of the most sensitive taste. The same remark is true of the style of Frederick Robertson, of Brighton ; nothing coming from his pen, as sermon, pamphlet or volume, that did not bear the mark of a master artist and seem to defy all attempts at improvement. Sir Joshua Reynolds, in his "Discourses on Art," evinced this architectural skill. Mrs. Browning, in her studies of Greek Dramatists, displayed nothing less than a genius for form, so that her first and most unstudied utterances were always her best. The illustrious French author, Pascal, in his "Provincial Letters," is second to no one of his countrymen in this respect; while such an American novelist as Hawthorne fascinates us as much by the unique aptness and delicacy of his diction as by any other literary quality.

We speak, thus, of a *finished* style, meaning, thereby, not simply that there is nothing omitted that should be included, but that what is included is wrought out with an exquisite sense of form. There is nothing approaching looseness, slovenliness or inelegance. In choice of topics ; in adjustment of plan ; in selection of diction ; in formation of sentences ; in the general tenor and movement of the discussion on to the end, there is manifest mastership in the art of expression as an art.

In no order of style does what is called, *culture*, so signally appear. We speak of literary culture, as distinct from that which is mental or ethical—that peculiar phase of individual taste which best expresses itself in the use of the pen. We speak of a style as classical, not only in the sense of standard, but in the further sense of finished. There is in such a style, what the best examples of Greek and Italian art evinced, a something exquisitely graceful, and, as such, gratifying to the eye and taste.

Nor are we speaking now, mainly, of poetry or poetical prose, in which it will be at once conceded that the literary style finds its most becoming and natural expression, but of prose in all its best and strongest forms; in history, biography and miscellany; in forensic and disputative writing—in forms, indeed, where it is the least expected. In Irving's "Life of Washington," in Lord Chesterfield's "Letters to His Son;" in Macaulay's "History of England;" in Lord's "Beacon Lights of History;" in Chateaubriand's "Genius of Christianity;" in the "Letters of Lady Mary Montagu;" in the pages of La Fontaine and Madame de Staël, we find this artistic element fully as pronounced as it is in Sir Philip Sidney's "Arcadia" or in the romances of the novelists.

Any one who has read or heard the best specimens of the pen of Wendell Phillips, such as his paper on "The Lost Arts," needs not to be told that delicacy and fineness of treatment reached therein their highest limit of excellence, as the reader found himself sitting spellbound and entranced under the weird-like witchery of the style, —so artless, yet so full of art; so natural, and yet so immeasurably above the possible attainment of others.

We have spoken of certain dangerous tendencies lying directly in the line of the style Intellectual. We encounter an equally dangerous tendency in the style Literary, in the temptation to extreme embellishment and attention to *form;* reducing all literature to Belles Lettres; subordinating the mental to the æsthetic, and making it our main ambition to become, in the South European sense, *littérateurs*, rather than robust and sturdy men of letters. Literatures, in almost every nation, have, at one time or another, yielded to this seductive influence, so that authors, such as Sidney and Donne, and Cowley and Blair, and even Macaulay himself, have, at times, substituted the means for the end, and carried the art of mere verbal execution beyond the limits of propriety. Here, again, the abuse of the law is its justification, and we restore the element of the æsthetic to its proper place in literary style when we mark it as a conspicuous element, and yet always in abeyance to the intellectual as supreme.

This leads us to what may be regarded as the

highest manifestation of the style before us. We refer to Literary Criticism. It is at this point, that we note the closest connection of the literary style with the intellectual, so that the highest type of the literary writer is the literary critic. This principle may be abundantly confirmed by a reference to some of the accepted critics of literary history. Longinus, in his treatise "On the Sublime;" Lessing, in his dissertations on "German Poetry and Greek Art;" Ruskin, in his "Stones of Venice" and similar discussions; Dryden, in his studies of classical and vernacular verse; Sainte-Beuve, of France, in his brilliant survey of authors and books—these and such as these were writers with regard to whom it would be difficult to state to which province they more properly belong, to the intellectual or the literary, and where they have done their greater work, in thought or in æsthetic art.

There are four or five names of modern eminence that occur to us as we write that illustrate, most fitly, what we mean by literary style applied to criticism. We refer to Matthew Arnold, of England, and to Mr. Whipple, Mr. Stedman and Mr. Lowell, of America, all of them intellectual authors and, yet, illustrious examples of literary skill in the sphere of criticism. Possessed of that ease of expression and dignity of manner so germane to the literary style, they especially exhibit that delicate finish of phrase and word which is its crowning charm, and this in closest union with a strong, vigorous order of thought. Rich in ideas and comprehensive in method, they are, none the less, in harmony with all the exactions of the most cultivated taste, and while they enlighten us, fascinate and satisfy us. Mr. Arnold's "Essays in Criticism;" Whipple's "American Literature" and "Eminent Men;" Mr. Stedman's "Victorian Poets" and "American Poets" and Mr. Lowell's prose papers, from his earliest production to his recent masterly oration at Harvard,—are a few examples of books best adapted to exemplify the highest type of the literary style as natural, noble, critical and finished and to beget, within the experience of the one who masters them, something of the same felicity of form.

To peruse such volumes thoroughly and appreciatively and not thereafter be more facile and finished in English utterance than before would seem to be impossible. This subject of the relation of style to criticism will receive fuller discussion.

METHODS OF CULTIVATION.

If we inquire, therefore, as to the best *methods* of cultivating the literary style and spirit we answer—

I. By Acquaintance with Literature—with what Mr. Arnold terms "the best that is known and thought in the world." The reference, here, is not to the acquisition of knowledge in general; to the fact that the writer should be a well-informed man on all topics pertaining to general scholarship and the affairs of men; but special stress must be laid upon that particular form of knowledge called literary, the aggregated product of the world's best literature. The literary style is based on literary authorship, as the intellectual style is based on intellectual authorship. The writer must be, in this sense, a man of books, fully at home in the literature of the past and present; conversant with the great authors of classical antiquity and with the equally distinguished names of Modern Continental Europe; with Cervantes, Lope de Vega, Racine, Petrarch, Schiller and, most especially, with the celebrated names of his own vernacular English. The English writer is to be so familiar with English literary history, that he may be said to have it at his command, in a sense not at all applicable to any other authorship; thoroughly imbued with the home feeling and with a laudable ambition to extend and defend the interests of his native speech.

There is, we may here remark, one particular branch of English Literature, especially designed to beget the English literary temper and style. We refer to English Literary Biography, whereby the careful reader comes into intimate relationship with the personality of authors; is enabled to look upon them and converse with them as personal friends, and to bring them, more and more, out of the region of the abstract into the open province of reality and life. No student can read such biographies as Spedding's "Life of Bacon;" Masson's "Life of Milton;" Lockhart's "Life of Scott;" Prior's "Life of Burke;" Trevelyan's "Life of

Macaulay;" Courthope's "Life of Addison;" or Holmes' "Life of Emerson" and not come into a closer contact with the literary habit and spirit of those authors than could possibly be obtained by the most conscientious perusal of their writings.

II. We note a second method of inducing such literary spirit and style in—Personal Familiarity with Literary Scenes, Places and Memorials—with the "Homes and Haunts of Poets," as Mr. Howitt has described them, in his charming volume on, "British Poets." We know of but few experiences which would so stir within the soul of an English student every literary element and motive as a month or two of travel through the British Isles, with the object of visiting the homes and schools and scenes and graves of Britain's greatest authors. A visit to the celebrated English Lake Country, where Coleridge and De Quincey lived awhile; where Wordsworth lived, at Rydal Mount, and where he lies buried in the old village yard at Grasmere; to stand by the tomb of Southey in Keswick; to walk out through the English leas from Eton College to Stoke Pogis, and stand in the old churchyard where Thomas Gray wrote his "Elegy" and where are his tomb and monument; to visit Dryburgh Abbey, where the great Sir Walter Scott is buried; to walk through the beautiful Ayrshire district and stop a while at the little peasant cottage in which Robert Burns was born and in which he penned his simple Scottish lyrics; to spend an hour, outside of Rome, in the Protestant Godsacre, and stand by the graves of Keats and Shelley, or to sit on the shore of the Bay of Spezzia, over whose waters Byron and Shelley sailed together and in whose depths Shelley found his grave; to walk through the halls of Trinity College, Dublin, where Edmund Burke was a student, and, so, on to the Cathedral where Dean Swift administered the rites of the church; to ride through the town of Auburn, of which Goldsmith so plaintively sings in his "Deserted Village;" above all, to walk along the lines of busts and memorials in Westminster Abbey, where lies the dust of England's greatest authors, from Chaucer to Coleridge and, in the village church at Stratford, to sit at the shrine of Shakespeare and think how Englishmen before us have written in prose and in verse—all this is nothing short of inspiring and stimulating to any sensitive literary nature, and kindles within him the unquenchable desire to do something, at least, in the line of his immortal predecessors, and worthy of his English name and lineage. There is a secret and an all-effective law of affinity and sympathy at work in such an experience as this, and we feel as we look upon such scenes as these, that it becomes us, and is binding upon us, to take up the work that these sons of song and masters of prose laid down and maintain the reputation of English Letters.

There is, yet, a more effective method—

III. Personal Contact with Living Authors.

This was one of the great occasions and offices of those literary clubs that flourished in the days of Elizabeth and Queen Anne and have, to some extent, existed in all distinctively literary eras. Whatever their social or political purposes may have been, their main design was to encourage authorship. Timid and rising authors came to these clubs with their latest and best work for criticism and consequent acceptance or rejection. Authors, old and young, compared notes and exchanged greetings; studied together the literary history of their time; watched with anxiety all signs of decadence, and hailed with delight every evidence of genuine literary progress. The Old Mermaid, of the days of Ben Jonson; and the October Club, of the days of Steele, were centres of literary influence second to none in the United Kingdom. Modern successors of these older organizations are established in London, Edinburgh, Boston and New York. Wits are sharpened thereby; sympathies kindled; errors corrected and excellencies encouraged,—in a word, literary taste and style are directly developed. The effect is altogether tonic and healthful. What Mr. Disraeli has called "The Amenities of Literature" are verified and expressed. The literary spirit, back of all book and pen and suggestive scene, is begotten and the way is widely opened for the best results for authorship.

These and kindred privileges will do more than

all other agencies combined to quicken within a writer whatever literary taste there is and to inspire the ever stronger ambition to develop it to fuller measure. He is to be congratulated whose earliest teachers were men of pronounced literary culture and able to impress, in a healthful way, their literary personality upon their pupils. The old English Universities are thus pervaded with literary life.

Cambridge, the seat of Harvard University, is especially fortunate in this regard, in that literature is there a fact as well as a theory, and Cambridge students aspiring to literary excellence have about them, in the persons of Holmes and Lowell, Childs and Norton, living exponents of literary art.

We note—That Modern English and American influences are as hostile to the Literary style as they are to the Intellectual. It must be confessed that, even in the best periods of our literature, this particular type of style has been far too limited in its expression. If Addison and Lamb and De Quincey possessed it, Swift and Ben Jonson did not; if Landor and Goldsmith and Burke and Macaulay possessed it, Bacon and Hooker, Hume and Gibbon and Carlyle did not, nor is it manifest, to any marked degree, in Thackeray and Bulwer and in such living authors as Froude and Freeman and McCarthy and our own venerable historian, Bancroft. Whatever these styles are, they are not literary; especially in the sense of being conspicuously natural and finished.

Any careful observer of the prevailing influences now at work in the mother country and at home will readily discern their anti-literary character. As the geologists would say, the *drift* or *trend* is toward the practical and commercial. Modern materialism is not confined to the schools as a metaphysical theory, but has assumed a wider scope, taking the form, far too largely, of a philosophy of life, the one incentive of all human activity. Trade, barter and profit; practical schemes and immediate results are the staple of conversation, and the main forms of individual and civic endeavor. All this has its value in certain directions, but is unfriendly, in the extreme, to the literary character and style. Not only have printers and publishers become more and more commercial in their callings, but authors themselves are inclined to make literary productions a question purely of supply and demand; profit and loss; so many pages for so much a page—and, ere we are aware, book-making, as it is called, is reduced to the level of a market transaction and all parties are satisfied.

The direct influence of such a procedure as this upon the rising generation of writers and upon our academic students, ambitious in authorship, is anything but helpful. Style, we are told, is worth what it will bring at the exchange. If the literary order of style has nothing to commend it but the fact that it is the expression of the finer and more cultivated side of one's nature, then must it be discarded in favor of something less refined but more remunerative.

Such is the undoubted tendency, and while there are writers who may be expected to yield to it, men of liberal training and culture should not, but by voice and pen oppose it. English and American authorship must be preserved among us in its literary purity and mental vigor. There are such qualities as dignity and finish and scholarly ease in style; commendable in themselves as elements of expression, quite independent of their relation to mercenary ends. Is there not some danger, we submit, as to loss of literary tone and character among us, in the existing ambition of authors and financial agents to reduce our best literature to a mere platform recital, more for the sake of the net proceeds at the door than for the sake of the literature itself, as a thing of beauty and of power! There is such a thing as culture in letters, the rich inheritance we have received from the literary past and which we in conscience are bound to maintain and transmit. Style postulates culture as it postulates thought, and has to do with a natural, dignified, facile and finished execution. It is the embodiment of thought in æsthetic and artistic forms; the distinctively literary type of intellectual life, in which, as in the temple of Jehovah at Jerusalem, beauty and strength are inseparably joined in one consummate product. Never more urgently than now have we needed, in English-speaking countries, this particular cast of authorship and style—the fusion of Norman ease and finish with Saxon sense and spirit ; of Roman smoothness and versatility of structure with Teutonic and Gothic vigor—that exquisite sweetness and grace of manner so signally exhibited in the old Knickerbocker school of Tuckerman and Morris and Willis and the incomparable Irving.

LITERARY STYLE.

Examples.

There was something in the temper of these celebrated men which secured them against the proverbial inconstancy both of the court and of the multitude. No intrigue, no combination of rivals, could deprive them of the confidence of their sovereign. No parliament attacked their influence. No mob coupled their names with any odious grievance. Their power ended only with their lives. In this respect, their fate presents a most remarkable contrast to that of the enterprising and brilliant politicians of the preceding and of the succeeding generation. Burleigh, was minister during forty years. Sir Nicholas Bacon held the great seal more than twenty years. Sir Walter Mildmay was Chancellor of the Exchequer twenty-three years. . . . They all died in office and in the enjoyment of public respect and royal favor. Far different had been the fate of Wolsey, Cromwell, Norfolk, Somerset, and Northumberland. Far different also was the fate of Essex, of Raleigh, and of the still more illustrious man whose life we propose to consider.—*Macaulay's "Essay on Lord Bacon."*

A man that is temperate, generous, valiant, chaste, faithful and honest may, at the same time, have wit, humor, mirth, good breeding and gallantry. While he exerts these latter qualities, twenty occasions migl.t be invented to show that he is master of the other noble virtues. Such characters would smite and reprove the heart of a man of sense, when he is given up to his pleasures. . . . He would see he has been mistaken all this while and be convinced that a sound constitution and an innocent mind are the true ingredients for becoming and enjoying life. All men of true taste would call a man of wit, who should turn his ambition this way, a friend and benefactor to his country; but I am at loss what name they would give him who makes use of his capacity for contrary purposes.—*Richard Steele's "Spectator" Papers.*

Age is the season of Imagination youth, of Passion; and having been long young, shall we repine that we are now old? They alone are rich who are full of years—the Lords of Time's Treasury are all in the staff of Wisdom; their commissions are enclosed in furrows in their foreheads and secured to them for life. Fearless of fate and far above fortune, they hold their heritage by the great charter of nature for behoof of all her children who have not, like impatient heirs, to wait for their decease; for every hour dispenses their wealth, and their bounty is not a late bequest but a perpetual benefaction. That Youth is the season of Passion, your own beating and bounding hearts now tell you—your own boiling blood. Intensity is its characteristic, and it burns like a flame of fire, too often but to consume. Your eyes are bright—ours are dim; but "it is the soul that sees" and their diurnal "sphere" is visible through the mist of tears. In that light, how more than beautiful—how holy appears even this world.—"*Recreations of Christopher North.*"

Will Wordsworth survive, as Lucretius survives, through the splendor of certain sunbursts of imagination refusing, for a passionate moment, to be subdued by the unwilling material in which it is forced to work, while that material takes fire in the working as it can and will only in the hands of genius, as it cannot and will not, for example, in the hands of Doctor Akenside? Is he to be known, a century hence, as the author of remarkable passages? Certainly a great part of him will perish, not, as Ben Jonson said of Donne, for want of understanding, but because too easily understood. His teaching, whatever it was, is part of the air we breathe. His finest utterances do not merely nestle in the ear by virtue of their music, but in the soul and life, by virtue of their meaning. Surely, he was not an artist, in the strictest sense of the word; neither was Isaiah; but he had a rare gift, the capability of being greatly inspired.—*Lowell's "Democracy.'*

CHAPTER III.

THE IMPASSIONED STYLE.

THERE are various names by which this order of style may be designated. We may call it the emotional, persuasive, fervid or forceful style; the cogent, effective or vivacious style; vital in its nature, method and results, and, as such, entering more or less fully into all departments of literature and writing. Differing, in some important particulars, from that type of style which we have termed intellectual, as, also, from that which is literary, it is supposed to have a sufficient degree of each of these representative orders to commend it to authors of ability and taste, while its relation to the style called popular is still more pronounced and important.

A brief examination of some of its expressions in the typical forms of authorship will evince the largeness of its province and function. We see it, most emphatically, in the best narration and description, whether such recitals and sketches be historical or feigned. In such works of fiction as

Hawthorne's "Scarlet Letter;" Kingsley's "Alton Locke" and "Two Years Ago;" in George Eliot's "Mill on the Floss" and Charlotte Brontë's "Jane Eyre;" in Dickens' Old Curiosity Shop," "Hard Times" and "David Copperfield;" in Bulwer's "Pompeii," Scott's "Heart of Mid-Lothian" and Thackeray's "Irish Sketches"—this life-like portraiture of men and things reaches, at times, the height of its excellence and assumes the appearance of reality itself. Within the domain of the actual and historical, this impassioned element naturally finds a full expression, as in Victor Hugo's description, in "Les Misérables," of the Battle of Waterloo; in Prescott's description of Mexican and Peruvian life; in Motley's stirring recital of the struggle in Holland for political freedom, as given us in his "John of Barnevelde;" in Macaulay's affecting account of the impeachment of Hastings, in the great hall of William Rufus, and, especially, in such volumes as Carlyle's "Cromwell" and "French Revolution." In these and similar authors, historical narrative and delineation rise far above the ordinary plane of fact and incident, and assume, for the moment, all the vividness and fervor of the most emotional address, and serve to awaken and energize and absorb us, as well as to instruct us.

So, in the province of argumentative and forensic writing, passion is seen in its best and most effective forms. It is probable, indeed, that there is no sphere of prose expression in which the emotive element has fuller sway and power. In the great historic debates and orations of Continental, English and American politics, as we have them reduced to written form, genuine feeling is seen at its climax, and we are not surprised to learn that the immediate results of their oral delivery were often overpowering. In such examples as Chatham's written oration "On the Right to Tax America;" Mackintosh's "On Behalf of Free Speech;" Lord Erskine's "On Limitation of Free Speech;" Richard Cobden's "On Protection;" Fox's "On Rejection of Napoleon's Overtures for Peace;" Edmund Burke's "On Resolutions for Conciliation with America;" Seward's "Irrepressible Conflict;" the efforts of Clay and Calhoun, Webster and Randolph, in the American Congress, or of Mirabeau, in the French Assembly—passion of thought and speech is the dominant quality,—so pronounced and potent as to carry all before it and effect its final purpose in the conscience and judgment of the reader. Even at this late date, though generations and centuries have elapsed since the first oral utterances of some of these deliberative and forensic efforts, our souls are stirred within us, as we read them, by the intensity of their fiery logic, and we seem to be standing in person within the very presence of these masters of speech.

In noting, more particularly, the salient characteristics of the Impassioned Style, we shall confine ourselves to three, as most distinctive.

I. The Element of Passion. It is this element, indeed, from which this special type of style derives its name and which, as such, must, first be considered. Milton's definition of poetry as "sensuous and passionate," would apply fully as appropriately to impassioned prose. It is that order of prose in which the heart is engaged as well as the thinking head or the designing hand; in which emotion is allied to conception and execution, and the vital impression of the reader is made, at the time, fully as important as his instruction, and far more important than his mere entertainment or pleasure. We speak, and speak correctly, of the heat of debate; of "thoughts that breathe and words that burn;" of the excitive and incitive elements in speech; of a style as animated, spirited, sanguine and magnetic—of an order of writing that seems to shine and flash and kindle as we peruse it. We may fittingly call it, the *lyric* element in prose expression; affecting us in its prose forms somewhat as we are affected by the most passionate elegiacs or pastorals of standard lyric verse; evoking within our deepest consciousness such phases and measures of genuine feeling as would be evoked by the recital of some of the choicest and tenderest odes of Moore and Collins and Burns. Such a style is suffused with this rich and sensuous idyllic quality. It reads as the most telling sonnets of Milton or Wordsworth read, and, for the time being, we surrender ourselves without reserve to its profound and governing influence.

More than this, there is nothing less than a *dramatic* or tragic element in the style before us, evincing itself, not infrequently, in those masterful productions wherein the emotion of the writer increases with the ever-deepening interest of his subject, until every line and word seems to palpitate with its presence. As the development of the idea goes on, there is a growth of feeling in the soul somewhat akin to the external progress of the tragedy from act to act and scene to scene. Each successive stage of its presentation becomes more emphatic and vivid and vital than the preceding, until, as we near the close, we discern that dramatic climax of thought and plan and motive and language which makes the completed product nothing less than electric in its impassioned effect upon the writer and the reader. Victor Hugo, in such a volume as "93," is a prose writer of this histrionic order; a veritable actor off the stage, with pen in hand, expressing his thought on paper so objectively as a living entity, that we see it and feel it and almost hear it as it speaks. There is, as we may say, a pulse in it whose regular and often violent throbbings we can discern, indicative of the great beating heart that lies imbedded at the centre of the author's life. All this is dramatic in its intensity, and as we are human and impressible, must move and master us at will.

As to the various *forms* in which such an emotion may express itself in style, we mark them as twofold; either in the line of the *tender* and pathetic, or in that of the *bold*, vehement and denunciatory. In such affectionate and affecting conferences as Charles Lamb held with his beloved sister Mary; or as Wordsworth held with his equally beloved Dorothy; in the gentle, reserved and touching essays of Irving and Goldsmith; in such impressive passages as Dickens' death of little Nell or Miss Mulock's scenes of domestic life; in the recorded interviews between Charlotte Brontë and her sisters Emily and Anne; in some of the scenes portrayed in Mrs. Stowe's "Uncle Tom," or in the sympathetic appeals of Helen Jackson on behalf of the ill-treated Indian—we note this manifestation of the passionate style on its plaintive and persuasive side; potent over us as we read it because so unassuming and delicate in its expression, gradually enlisting our interest and sympathies as the narative goes on, until we sit entranced and captivated.

Most of the Shakespearean female characters, as Mrs. Jameson has so beautifully presented them, illustrate this softer and sweeter type of feeling, while in the spacious realm of English fiction Sir Walter Scott has furnished us with feminine characters, not a few, in whom this gentleness of person and manner has assumed its most fascinating forms.

Of the more declarative and open type of the impassioned in style, literary history has abundant examples. We see it in the trenchant Ciceronian orations against Catiline; in the fiery Philippics of Demosthenes; in the almost unearthly utterances of the great Italian Savonarola, as he contended for the purity of the church of his day; in the intrepid attacks of Luther upon the papacy and his matchless deliverances at the Diet of Worms; in the spoken and written words of the dauntless John Knox; in the heated language of Gambetta, the great Gallic diplomat; in the almost withering invectives of Garrison and Wendell Phillips, in their courageous defence of the abolition of slavery—in a word, in all those recorded utterances in which, from time to time, the defenders of vital principles and ideas have taken their lives in their hands, and under the deepest convictions of the truth and their missions to the world, have written what they have written in tears and blood. Such men have written passionately because they have thought and lived and worked passionately, with the deepest intensity of which their natures were capable, if so be their language might find its way past all opposition and affront, into the most secret and interior convictions of men. Such an order of style, provided it be under the safe control of judgment, and not offensive to literary taste, is, in its place, as representative as any, and as needful, and, in one or other of its forms, as reserved or outspoken, must find a place in all effective address.

If it be asked, at this point, how such a measure of feeling may be secured by the writer, we answer, that, personal temperament apart, nothing will so readily and fully induce it, as the continuous *study* of scenes and events calculated to elicit it in its varied phases of pity, sympathy, indignation and enthusiasm. The practical results of such a method are strikingly exhibited in the history of the great Crusades of the Middle Ages, when the hundreds of thousands of valiant warriors who marched under their leaders to the rescue of the Holy Sepulchre from the ravages of the infidels were incited to such bravery and perils by their protracted contemplation of those indignities of which the cross of Christ was made the subject. We may say, in the language of the Psalmist, that "their heart was hot within them." While they were "musing the fire burned"—the fire of passion, of holy indignation and holy enthusiasm, insomuch that they rose from their meditations ready to march and to suffer, to fight and to perish, in the defence of the truth and the cross. Meditation upon impassioned objects and incidents is the fruitful mother of passion in our own souls, and when once awakened, must, despite all opposition, manifest itself in word and act.

Hence, the reading of what may be called, the literature of feeling, is in the direct line of the education of such feeling. No writer in the formation of his style, however lethargic his nature, can studiously peruse the best specimens of emotional narrative, description, argument and oration, as they exist in English Letters, and not feel their quickening influence.

"Certainly I must confess," writes Sir Philip

Sidney in his "Apologue," "I never heard the old song of Percy and Douglas that I found not my heart moved more than with a trumpet." So, also, will he feel who hears or reads the words of those who have said what they have said from the innermost depths of their hearts, in order to reach and affect the heart of others. "Passion," writes Shakespeare, "is catching."

The impassioned style, we may add, is "catching." It passes by an instinctive process from orator to hearer; from author to reader, and as others weep or laugh, denounce or praise, we speak and act in common with them. It is the philosophical law of natural affinity and of mutual influence applied in the province of literature and style. If, as Doctor Johnson tells us—"Whoever wishes to attain an English style, familiar and elegant must give his days and nights to the study of Addison," so, may we say, in the light of our present discussion, that—Whoever wishes to attain an English style, impressive and impassioned, must spend his days and nights with such intensive authors as Milton and De Quincey, Burke and Carlyle, Patrick Henry and Daniel Webster.

II. The Element of Personality. This is an element common to all the species of style—intellectual, literary and popular—and, yet, especially adapted to the style Impassioned. If, as we are told, the style is the man, then, in the style before us, the human or personal element is more conspicuous than in any other. It is a style in which, as in no other, there is the fullest external revelation of the inner man. So pronounced is this individual element in the written expression of thought and life, that there is a racial and national personality in literature clearly visible along the line of the world's great civilizations. In North European countries, as in Germany and Denmark, this assumes a distinctive type, as vigorous, rugged and undemonstrative ; while in all South European countries, literary personality, as national personality, is impassioned. Hence, the style is full of what might be called a tropical fervor, so that in prose and poetry, in social life and common speech, all is expressive and emotional. No French philosopher illustrates such a passionate personality in his style more happily than Monsieur Cousin. Whether in his metaphysical, ethical or miscellaneous discussions, there is the same Gallic vivacity and spirit. In his attractive treatise on" The True and the Beautiful" deep æsthetic sensibility could scarcely be more pronounced and sympathetic. He writes as if in love with truth and beauty; so as to regard them with Keats, as one and the same inner quality of life and of letters. VictorHugo, in fiction, and Madame de Staël, in general literature, exemplify a similar intensity and purity of feeling ; while Fenelon, in his "Telemaque" and Pascal, in his "Thoughts" and "Provincial Letters", always write from the innermost recesses of their natures, and thus write emotionally. The same order of expression is seen in that impressive correspondence maintained among the members of the Port Royal School of pietists, in which Jansenism took the form of what has well been called a Calvinistic Catholicism, and these devoted souls poured forth their personal feeling in the most ardent strains possible to their vernacular. The same is true of Petrarch, Dante and Tasso in Italy; of Calderon and Lope de Vega in Spain and Portugal, respectively; in a word, of all those romance writers who by reason of climate and national temper spoke and wrote and acted feelingly.

If we compare the different sections of the British Isles with this idea before us, the results are equally striking. The personality of the Scotch, the Irish and the Welsh is demonstrative and emotional, as distinct from that of the English, which is more cautious and reserved. We have but to open at random the pages of Knox, Melville, Rutherford, O'Connor, Grattan, Swift, Goldsmith, Burke and Chalmers to find the presence of the impassioned pervading the lines and the letters. All is expressive and impressive, in turn, thrilling and touching, fervent and fiery, and often overwhelming; enlisting, at once, the profoundest mental and ethical sympathies of the reader, and begetting in him a passion similar to theirs. These writers are all men of heart, experiencing what they write before they write it, and, often, carrying the convictions of their readers and auditors by the simple persuasiveness of passion.

It is highly probable, if not, indeed, historical, that there is no extant prose in any literature that may be said to be so saturated and surcharged with true emotive energy and individuality as the old Celtic prose. Possessed of comparatively little æsthetic grace, it is heated through and through with the inner fire of feeling, and vivifies us as we peruse it. Armies have been made victorious and great national movements furthered by its irresistible force, while, to this day, to him who is able to interpret them, those ancient British masterpieces are full of a "fine frenzy," and awaken the deepest responses of the soul. The same principle holds, to a limited extent, in our own country, where the typical specimens of Southern argumentative or forensic prose are the choicest examples of passion on the side of personality. John C. Calhoun, of South Carolina, or Henry Clay, of Kentucky, superbly illustrate this tropical intensity of thought and address.

Hence, one of the best methods of cultivating the impassioned style is, by developing *personality of character*, discussion and belief. However dependent the writer may be and must be on others, he must also be, in the best sense, independent of all external opinion; being, first and last, himself, and insisting on doing his own thinking. There is a sense in which every student and exponent of style must write *ex cathedra*—with personal and plenary authority, holding himself amenable to no higher laws than those of revealed truth itself and the finally accepted results of general opinion. True pas sion in literature cannot coexist with the cringing, time-serving, slavish spirit. It must have air and space and freedom in which to vegetate and flourish. What is termed force of character is simply the intense expression of one's personality, and that involves courage, the attainment of the truth by individual methods, and a tenacious maintenance of the truth, increasing in its tenacity in proportion to the strength of the opposition. When Webster addressed the United States Senate on the Constitution and the Union; or Calhoun defended, in his inimitable way, the Nullification Doctrine, or Charles Sumner uttered his burning words on The Civil Rights Bill—there was passion in the style, and passion because of personality. These eminent advocates of their respective theories had lived along their own lines; done their own thinking; had a message for the people, reached by them through independent methods, and believed by them to be desirable and feasible, and the result, in each case, was nothing less than dramatic as to the intensity of interest that was evoked. The style, as it went on, passed from one degree of warmth unto another, on through the stage of ardent feeling to red heat and to white heat, melting and fusing whatever, at the time, came in contact with it. Personality is not always emotional, but no emotion can exist without it.

III. The third and final element of the style before us is, Power. It is, by way of special quality, the effective or emphatic style—an order of style by which definite and, often, immediate results are accomplished. It may be said, indeed, that feeling, in its very nature, is forcible. There is in its very composition an impelling or a propelling factor, making it, thereby, more or less potent over all that it affects. Thomas De Quincey is fond of calling attention to the Literature of Knowledge and the Literature of Power, and of exalting this second type. We are here dealing with a literature of power—the power arising from the passion in the soul of the writer, and, as Webster would insist, also in the subject and the occasion. We speak, in this sense, of a nervous style; of a masterful style, possessed of what Dr. Chalmers has called "expulsive power." There is a general progress under it from beginning to end which might be called—its momentum. Like a mighty river, fed by numerous tributaries, it gathers volume, velocity and power as it advances, until, at the end, it may be as irresistible as a great tidal wave. It is, in the best sense, impulsive, intensive and projective, marked by the presence of that "*vis vivida*" that gives to all style its potential character. One of De Quincey's miscellaneous papers is suggestively styled "Suspiria de Profundis" —breathings from the depths. All truly impassioned writing is of this subterranean order—welling up from the lowermost levels of the nature of the writer and therefore influential over others. The diction, structure, method and figure—all are cogent and convincing. There is the evident presence of mastery throughout. The author is in dead earnest and living earnest in what he is penning. He cannot express himself otherwise and be true to his deepest instincts and experiences. His feelings can neither be feigned nor repressed, and what he pens becomes, thereby, an active agency in literature and the life of the world.

It is very suggestive to note that the highest form of this impassioned power in style is in connection with the principle of *ethical earnestness*, that profound movement of soul which is nothing less than an upheaval of the entire sentient nature, and before whose uprising and ongoing nothing can successfully stand.

It is for this reason among others that within the sphere of sacred and pulpit prose some of the most effective results on record have been reached. Old Hugh Latimer, in the days of Henry VIII., wrote such an order of prose—potential from introduction to conclusion, and causing every guilty conscience whom it addressed to see its guilt as never before, and to confess it. This was the style which Richard Baxter used at Kidderminster; which Dr. Barrow and Bishop South employed in the stormy days of the Revolution and Great Rebellion; which the eloquent Gallic preacher Saurin used at the Hague, and which, in the hands of the American Edwards, lifted men fairly off their feet by the cogency of its appeals. . . . It was in this impassioned and effective manner that the Reformers of the sixteenth century wrote and preached to princes and worldly prelates against their public and private sins. So thundered the lion-hearted Luther in the presence of German Barons, while it will ever remain as the signal glory of the great French preachers of the seventeenth century—of Massillon and Bossuet and Bourdaloue, that, when at many other European courts, the royal ear was filled with ill-timed eulogiums, these courageous men stood up at the very centre of Parisian profligacy and warned the great monarch and his courtiers against prevailing sins.

So is it outside the special province of sacred address, that such ethical earnestness is seen to be effective—especially in the discussion and enforcement of principles whose basis, significance and objects are ethical ; having to do with some important social, political or educational question. Dr. Eliphalet Nott, in his masterly address "On the Death of Alexander Hamilton," evinced this species of impassioned power. Charles Sumner, in his speech on the Kansas-Nebraska Bill, evinced it, as did Calhoun, On the Slavery Question ; Webster against Hayne ; Beecher in Exeter Hall, London, in defence of the American War Policy ; Mirabeau and Gambetta in the French Assembly ; and, most conspicuously of all, those fiery leaders of the Crusades, such as Peter of Amiens, Pope Urban II. and Innocent III., and Bernard of Clairvaux, who by the magic and the might of their intensive address moved the multitudes before them on to the wars, and made it appear, at the time, that the failure on the part of any loyal subject to take up arms against the cruelties of the Saracens and the desecrators of the Cross was treason alike before God and man, and would be visited with the most condign punishment. During what is called the War of Liberation, in Germany, when deliverance from the tyranny of Napoleonic rule was the one desire of all others, orators spoke and writers wrote in this emotive and cogent manner; partly, because, in the deep intensity of their convictions, they could not have done otherwise, and, partly, because it was through this particular method of appeal that they hoped to be the more potent and persuasive. The object was an immediate effect, and the method was effective, and nothing of the nature of the impotent and inert could for one moment be entertained, in the face of the pressing necessities of the times.

It was a time when some were fighting and some were writing and haranguing. The sword and the pen were both busily at work, but back of the warrior were the writer and the herald, inciting the people to take up arms and not to lay them down till victory was assured. The events and interests were stirring and the style of the time was correspondingly stirring. The pen was a power.

1. We note, in closing, that the Impassioned Style has existed, as an historical element, in all leading literatures and periods, and should have place, in some substantial form, in the style of

every writer and in every species of discourse, secular or sacred. It is one of the few radical types of style, demanded, in part, by the very nature of the style itself, and, in part, by the presence of that indifference, prejudice and hostility to the truth which demand for their removal something more than an insipid, enervating type of expression. The intellectual style may reach and affect the judgments of men. It will not, necessarily, arouse and impel them to right action, on any given issue that is presented. The literary style may reach and affect their tastes, and rest at that point, as having fulfilled its mission. An additional and a different order of appeal must be made, before malice and bigotry and stupidity give way, in turn, to good will, impartial candor and personal interest. Instruction and entertainment must be supplemented and reinforced by intense impression. In such necessities, style must assert its more pronounced and positive qualities ; must become pungent, penetrating and searching ; breaking in pieces all that is callous ; burning its way as a fire from heaven through all defilement and dross out into the open field of purity. Its language must be true and telling ; its method, direct and ingenuous ; its spirit fearless, and its final object the maintenance of the truth.

As all the lower forms of literature, as seen in fiction and journalism, poetry and miscellany, take advantage of this impassioned principle, and press it successfully to the dangerous extremes of the sensual and debasing, so much the more must all higher literature accept it and utilize it for worthiest ends, exhibiting, thereby, a realism of the spirit as Rousseau and Rabelais; Tolstöi and Zola; Ouida and Renan exhibit a "realism of the flesh."

2. Such an effective order of style, we may add, is especially to be pressed in the presence of scholars and students, so inclined to underrate and discard it, and the tendency of whose pursuits, as introspective and didactic, is somewhat calculated to weaken its influence among them. Though the intellectual style is the first order of style for scholars and for all men, and though the literary style, must be regarded as of high value, this is not to say of impassioned writing that it is inferior in its nature and makes no vital appeal to the interest of students. Of the great representative orders of prose expression, it takes its place as one, and cannot yield that place. Writers who are to be, in the best sense of the term, successful must be emotive, possessed of that passion and personality and power, which make up the essential unity of the impassioned style. They must write what they write, out of their own hearts into the hearts of others. They must dip their pens, not infrequently, into the open fountain of human experiences and sympathies, and write impressively as well as clearly and tastefully and popularly.

We have spoken of the danger of undue abstruseness and formality along the line of the style intellectual as, also, of the danger of a haughty æstheticism along the line of the style literary, of each of which extremes no better preventive could be found than that quality of expression now before us, in its honest, unaffected and forcible utterances. We deem it eminently safe to say that much of the best efforts in authorship of our educated men is lost by reason of its lack of these cogent elements of expression. Intelligible and in good taste, there is an important something that it lacks and that is—impassioned vitality—an internal and external potency of character that would sensibly affect us as we came into its presence and, often, thrill us through and through.

In a word, all true style is stirring and stimulative ; warming and firing the soul of the reader as he scans it ; quickening within his dormant being every worthiest faculty and feeling, leaving his soul all aglow with light and heat, with faith and love and holy courage. There is such a thing as an eloquent style, as it stands upon the paper in its unspoken form, instinct with true passion, with the author's deepest personality and power. We can almost see it move and hear it speak. It is filled to the full with what the French call—unction—permeated to its core with the very principle of life ; inspiring in its effect upon us, as if it were the product of a special divine afflatus, and never more urgently needed at any time than now—to add heat to light ; to convert desire into volition ; to impress the truth indelibly upon the minds of men and to make of men of letters, the world over, what they of right ought to be—men of power over others. In fine, style, at this point, is an inspiration. It is the outbreathing to others of the divine inbreathing into us. It is the expression of impression—the natural outflow of that within us which is supernatural—the embodiment in written form of what Mr. Emerson has suggestively called—"the Over-Soul."

THE IMPASSIONED STYLE.

Examples.

If it be desired to know the immediate cause of all this free writing and free speaking, there cannot be assigned a truer than your own mild and free and humane government; it is the liberty, Lords and Commons, which your own valorous and happy counsels have purchased us; liberty which is the nurse of all great wits; this is that which has enlightened and rarefied our spirits like the influence of heaven; this is that which hath enfranchised, enlarged and lifted up our apprehensions degrees above themselves. Ye cannot make us now less capable, less knowing, less eagerly pursuing of the truth, unless ye first make yourselves, less the lovers, less the founders of our true liberty. Give me the liberty to know, to utter and to argue freely, according to conscience, above all liberties.—*Milton's " Areopagitica."*

Gentlemen, I have had my day. I can never sufficiently express my gratitude to you for having set me in a place, wherever I could lend the slightest help to great and laudable designs. If I have had my share, in any measure giving quiet to private property and private conscience; if by my vote I have aided in securing to families the best possession, peace; if I have joined in reconciling kings to their subjects and subjects to their prince. . . . I have not lived in vain. I do not here stand before you accused of venality or of neglect of duty. It is not said that, in the long period of my service, I have, in a single instance, sacrificed the slightest of your interests to my ambition or to my fortune. No, the charges against me are all of one kind, that I have pushed the principles of general justice and benevolence too far; further than a cautious policy would warrant.—*Burke's Speech to the Electors of Bristol.*

That the British infantry soldier is more robust than the soldier of any other nation can scarcely be admitted by those who, in 1815, observed his powerful frame, distinguished amidst the united armies of Europe. . . . It has been asserted that his undeniable firmness in battle is the result of a phlegmatic constitution uninspired by moral feeling. Never was a more stupid calumny uttered. Napoleon's troops fought in bright fields, where every helmet caught some beams of glory, but the British soldier conquered under the cold shade of aristocracy. No honors awaited his daring, no despatch gave his name to the applause of his countrymen; his life of danger and hardship was uncheered by hope, his death unnoticed. Did his heart sink, therefore? The result of a hundred battles and the united testimony of impartial writers of different nations have given the first place amongst the European infantry to the British.—*Sir William Napier's "War in the Peninsula."*

Advance then, ye future generations. We would hail you as you rise in your long succession, to fill the places which we now fill. We bid you welcome to this pleasant land of the fathers. We bid you welcome to the healthful skies and the verdant fields of New England. We greet your accession to the great inheritance which we have enjoyed. We welcome you to the blessings of good government and religious liberty. We welcome you to the treasures of science and the delights of learning. We welcome you to the immeasurable blessings of rational existence, the immortal hope of Christianity and the light of everlasting truth.—*Daniel Webster's Plymouth Oration.*

CHAPTER IV.

THE POPULAR STYLE.

THIS fourth division of style is popular, as distinct from the style intellectual or literary or impassioned. It is not meant by this that it is altogether unintellectual or unliterary or unemotional, but that it is not distinctly marked by any one of these characteristics. Some degree of mental excellence, as of literary and persuasive excellence, it must possess, in order to be assigned a place among the prominent classes of English style. It has, however, qualities other than these, and more conspicuous, by reason of which it is termed popular. Not to be confounded with that order of expression which we call scholarly, or with that which is notably finished and fervent, it still has enough of these features somewhat to commend it to scholars and authors, and yet is a style primarily designed for the people as such, in their corporate capacity as the body politic and social—the great Middle Class of the English and American public. It may rightfully be called—

The Style of the Commonalty of every country; appealing not so much to either of the extremes of modern populations—the upper and learned ranks, or the lowermost, illiterate orders—but to the intelligent, average classes as they exist among us.

There are, as we are well aware, two distinct senses of the word popular—the higher and the lower; the one, as seen in the widely read and deservedly current fiction of the great British Novelists of the days of Dickens: the other, even more widely read, despite its mental and moral inferiority, as seen in the romances of Smollett and Aphra Behn, and in much of the miscellaneous literature of the day. To this latter and lower order of style we shall refer in the sequel. We speak, at present, of style as popular in the best sense of the word—of a grade of authorship composed for the people; originating out of their deepest and strongest needs; presented by authors conversant with such needs and in fullest sympathy with them; presented in a manner best adapted to meet the common want, and never failing to elevate popular thought by successive gradations to the level of what is noble and commendable.

A brief examination of the radical features of this style will reveal its true character and its manifest difference from any other type of expression with which it might be confounded.

I. It is, first of all, an Intelligible Style. We may speak of it, in good First English phrase, as understandable. If clearness of conception and presentation is the very first requisite of all successful writing, whatever the form, method or motive of the writing, it is pre-eminently so as to the style before us. What is called the popular embodiment of ideas, in distinction from their philosophic or artistic embodiment, is based on the law of perspicuity. What is said to the great body of any nation in its organic or collective capacity must be said in terms as clear as crystal, shining in their own light, almost axiomatic in their plainness. What is written, as we say, for the masses, quite unused to libraries and schools of learning and logical processes, must be so written that it may be taken in at a glance. As soon as the eye sees it, the mind is to apprehend it and be able, thenceforth, to utilize it. It must be, in this respect, like to the gospel message—so clear and plain, that a "wayfaring man, though a fool, need not err therein;" so that "he who runs may read." One of Mr. Arnold's favorite words, "lucidity," or, as he elsewhere terms, it, "light," applies here. In choice of words; in form of statement; in adjustment of facts, and in general process to the end—all must be lucid and luminous—full of light and dispensing light.

How signally such a feature appears in the writings of Bunyan, the great Christian allegorist; of De Foe, the historic founder of the secular

English Novel; and in those of Jonathan Swift, the famous literary dean of the Dublin Cathedral! We know, as a matter of accepted fact, that, next to "King James' Version of the English Bible" and the "Prayer Book" of the Anglican Church, the three books of our literature containing the largest percentage of native terms are the three great books of these respective authors—"Pilgrim's Progress," "Robinson Crusoe" and "Gulliver's Travels." No three books can be mentioned in English or any other literature that have been more conspicuously popular and, largely, by reason of their verbal transparency. The common reader can at once see into them and through them. The reading of them is indeed the understanding of them. If they are re-read, as they so often are, it is not the better to apprehend the sense, but the more fully to enjoy the teaching. There are few ambiguous phrases or complex structures or abstruse analyses or obscure reasonings or hidden motives; all is above board, an honest and an ingenuous unbosoming of the heart of the author to win and subdue the heart of the reader. Mrs. Stowe's "Uncle Tom" may be cited as a very close rival of these three famous books; not merely because of its graphic delineation of slave life in the days of American slavery, but, also, by the charm of its verbal clearness. The language and the style are purposely brought down from the upper grade of society to the level of the average mind, and the people are surprised to find that there is nothing in this simple narrative of fact so involved and obscure that they cannot, at once, apprehend and enjoy it. Oliver Goldsmith wrote his essays, poems, his "Vicar of Wakefield" and histories of Rome and England and "Animated Nature" in this unadorned and severe simplicity of phrase and manner. Bayard Taylor, of our own country, has ever evinced, as a narrator of travels, this enviable clearness of idea and expression, so that in such volumes as, "Views Afoot," "Eldorado" "A Voyage on the Nile," "The Lands of the Saracens," "At Home and Abroad," and similar sketches, the reader has scarcely to think at all, but simply to submit himself to the course of the history as it runs, and be carried by it pleasantly on from event to event and from scene to scene. Richard Steele, in the pages of the "Spectator," penned his weekly papers to the English public with this openness of style. Quaint Thomas Fuller, in his "English Worthies," used this same translucent diction, while our own genial-natured Irving has no superior in secular letters as a writer whose first statements are as clear as the last; who wrote plainly because he thought plainly and had no other object in writing his biographies, sketches, essays and histories than that his readers should see at once his meaning and be profited thereby. What shall be said, in this connection, of the simple-hearted Izaak Walton, author of "The Complete Angler" or "The Contemplative Man's Recreation" as, also, of the Lives of Donne, Hooker, Herbert and Wotton! The historian Hallam is undoubtedly correct when he speaks of these volumes as defying all imitation in the line of a child-like and an unaffected charm of manner.

In this respect, the popular style is second to none in its conditions and its value, in that its first essential is the first characteristic of all acceptable style. In this respect, all authors, however intellectual or literary or forceful, should sit at the feet of the deservedly popular writer, if so be they may be sure that what they write is, first of all, understandable. If not so, it is unphilosophical, unliterary and useless.

II. We note a further feature of the style before us, in that it is Timely and Practical. The popular style must deal with what Dr. Holland was wont to call "Topics of the Time;" with what the general public are pleased to call—living issues. There is an ever-more emphatic protest, on the part of common readers, against the visionary, abstruse and unpractical in literature. The province of fiction apart, in which the unreal is understood to be the staple of material, readers are clamorously calling for a business-like, an every-day order of prose writing; marked by the presence of current questions, discussed in the modern, unconventional spirit, and having reference to ends specifically local and immediate. It is the same desire in our day that marked the promiscuous public of Addison's time, as they quickly appreciated his endeavor to bring philosophy from the clouds and closets down and out to the club-rooms and counting-rooms of the world. The main reason why the "Spectator," "Freeholder," "Guardian," "Tatler," "Rambler" and other serials were so widely circulated and accepted is seen in the fact, that their topics were always germane to the status of English society at the time. They said little about the age of Chaucer or that of Henry VIII., but a great deal about the Augustan age; said but little of the factions, frivolities, politics and pursuits of Elizabethan and Stuart England, but aimed their arrows, in every instance, at the targets exposed in the reign of Queen Anne.

It is quite noticeable that, intellectual in his thought and style as was Lord Bacon, he adapted himself in his essays to what he understood to be the legitimate demands of current issues. As he tells us in his Preface, he appealed directly "to men's business and bosoms," and, in the discussion of such themes as, Friendship, Studies, Empire, Ambition, Fortune and The Vicissitude of Things, kept his philosophic eye on the events transpiring in the 16th century and, thus, wrote for his contemporaries, as well as for "times succeeding."

It may, indeed, be affirmed that periodical literature, as a distinctive type, has largely, for this reason, been, in all nations, a popular type; popular because periodical, changing its themes and purposes with the ever-varying changes of the time, and awakening, at the outset, the common interest of the common mind.

In this feature of practicality or timeliness there is nothing necessarily intellectual or literary. In fact, there is a sense in which this purely visible and tangible order of prose, this mercantile manner of choosing and discussing topics with primary reference to present ends, is quite averse to any high degree of mental and artistic excellence. Subjects more philosophic and abstract call forth the larger faculties and admit of a more thorough, comprehensive and dignified discussion.

Still, here again there need be no specific conflict. The popular style has its place and office, as others have theirs. In its proper sphere, it is desirable, as it insists that writers must, at times, discard the scientific and technical and deign to descend to the middle and even lower grades of society, and talk to men in the language in which they were born. The most gifted of authors ought to be able, occasionally, at least, to step down from their habitual altitude of high discussion to what Dr. Chalmers has significantly called "the ground floor" of human life, and, if not able to do so, to encourage by every possible way those practical and versatile authors who are willing, perchance, to surrender their personal ambitions in the line of exalted authorship in order to reach and affect those teeming millions of their fellows who live on or below the dead level of human life and need an uplifting hand. Dr. Chalmers, of Scotland, was himself a remarkable example of this self-surrendering spirit in authorship, discoursing, as he did, at one hour, to the choicest minds of the Scottish capital, and, in the next, addressing the gathered crowds, even from the slums of the city, on the most practical questions that could engage them—on health and cleanliness and common morals.

III. A further mark of the Popular Style is, its Method as Flexible and Graphic. The importance of this special feature can scarcely be overstated. Next to clearness, it is the most radical element in the popular presentation of thought. We may best express our meaning by saying—that the popular style does not assume to have any method that is binding on the writer. Its unique personality as a style lies in the fact, that it is unmethodical without being immethodical; follows no plan presented by others, and follows no one plan of its own in any two consecutive efforts. It rather prides itself in being unscholarly in its method. It makes a point of reducing the logical element to a minimum, if not, indeed, of eliminating it, lest the average reader may discern it and be repelled. It would not be amiss to call it, the purely extempore style of writing, as distinct from that which is studied and in which the author is supposed to follow an order of procedure more or less pre-arranged.

In this respect, the popular style is descriptive, delineative and pictorial, rather than close or consecutive. Bound to no pre-established law, logical or literary, it becomes a law unto itself. Abandoning itself, therefore, to the leading impulses of the hour, it goes hither and thither only because of a happy combination of occurrences, and is as willing to go in one direction as in another, provided that there be the conspicuous absence of constraint and logical sequence. It is a style that is, out and out, discursive and desultory, leaping about from point to point in the veriest caprice of movement, not desirous of tarrying long enough at any one position to examine it minutely or endanger the interest of the reader. It makes a special study of variety, point and pertinence; discards all polysyllables and debatable issues, and dreads nothing so much as the annoyance that arises from the prosaic or the prolix in the appearance of overmuch learning. What Mr. Rees has phrased "The Pleasures of a Bookworm," or Mr. Lang, "Letters to Dead Authors," such a style fails to appreciate, as it strictly discards everything that savors of the study, the cloister and the tomb. It is the chatty, colloquial style of coffee-houses and drawing-rooms; of lobby-chambers and leisurely retreats—the talk of the shop, the market, the street and the exchange reduced to writing. It hails with delight every evidence on the part of its patrons that it is as free as the air in its province; unrestricted as a school-boy in its whims and ways; absolutely under no condition of phrase or form save as the passing question of the moment may engage its attention.

We are speaking of the popular style on its

better side, and must be on our guard against condemning it because of its elasticity of method. If it has no plan, it pretends to have none, and is content to justify such absence by the increasing presence of those equally desirable results which it secures by reason of its unrestraint. Such an author as Robert L. Stevenson, at present so prominently before the American public, will happily illustrate all the characteristic features of the style in question, and, most especially, this endless diversity or liberty of method. In his various works, such as "The New Arabian Nights," "Virginibus Puerisque," "Memoirs and Portraits," "Familiar Studies of Men and Books," and similar collections, though he, at times, tells us that a certain thread is visible that binds these papers together, it is, often, in vain that we look for the logical thread. A volume means, in no sense, the connected discussion of a carefully chosen topic, or even the unified presentation of related topics, but an off-hand assemblage of a dozen papers on a dozen unrelated themes. In any one paper, taken by itself, the subject indicated at the outset, if indeed any is indicated, is glanced at rather than developed. There is no attempt at development. The writer regards the caption simply as a point at which, now and then, to aim, according to his fancy. He feels himself as much at liberty to miss it as to hit it. The paper is a series of comments, extemporized for the occasion; some of them, appropriate; some of them, irrelevant—a series of digressions from the point at issue, and often, as in the case of Swift, digressions from digressions. Having taken his text, as the exegete would, he often takes immediate leave of it, and the result is, a discursion or an excursion, called, by way of literary compliment, an article. Paradox is made a staple commodity. The assertion of one line modifies and, perhaps, nullifies that of the preceding. Novel and startling opinions are broached simply for their novelty, and, ere we are aware, curiosity is so confirmed into a habit that the ordinary becomes "stale, flat and unprofitable," and we crave the rare and racy. Such authoresses as Kate Field, Fanny Fern and Gail Hamilton are of this discursive order. Mr. Boyd, in his "Country Parson," "Leisure Hours" and "Every-Day Philosopher," illustrates it. Mr. Bissell, in his "Obiter Dicta," touches on Truth, Humbug, Falstaff, Book-buying and on well-known authors with this literary abandon of all established form. Such a living novelist as Frank Stockton, in his "Rudder Grange," "Roundabout Rambles" and "Tales out of School," leads us in this free and easy manner, quite unconcerned as to where and how. In such a style, the graphic and picturesque abound. All is sparkling, sprightly, crisp and attractive—a kind of out-of-door strolling, with hat in hand, through a beautiful landscape, where all is light and life and gayety. The method is panoramic.

In a word, the popular style must be *entertaining* in order to verify its right to exist, and whatever element of instructiveness or æsthetic and emotive interest it may possess, it aims, first and last, to attract and enchain attention. Its final purpose is recreative, and the farther it can separate itself from the precincts of the school, the better. Hence, it deals largely in the humorous and burlesque; seasons its pages with well-selected satire, and thus engages the sympathy of the reader by its good-natured attacks on men and things, on prevailing faults and follies. There is, indeed, no phase of current opinion or habit on which it does not feel itself at liberty to touch. The style of Sidney Smith and of Charles Lamb was, in this sense, popular. Mrs. Charles, in her brilliant "Chronicles of the Schönberg-Cotta Family," is a conspicuous example of this type. Such works as Martin Luther's or Coleridge's "Table Talk;" Howitt's "Visits to Remarkable Places;" Wilson's "Bryant and His Friends;" Irving's "Sketch Book;" John Brown's "Rab and His Friends;" Hazlitt's "Miscellanies;" Dickens' "Christmas Stories;" Dobson's "Eighteenth Century Essays" and Dr. Holmes' "Autocrat of the Breakfast Table" are in this clear, flexible and practical vein: happy in conception and execution; plastic and pictorial in form and always entertaining. Such informal and friendly correspondence as Göethe held with Schiller, or Fenelon with Madame Guyon, exhibits this colloquial freedom of vein and manner.

The popular style is and must be readable—plain enough to be readable, and practical and flexible enough to be read. This is its unique feature and ultimate aim. Style may be this or that in its purpose, or accomplish this or that in its results. It is not popular unless it is so presented as to command the actual attention of the great reading public. If it is for them, they will, by an unerring instinct, detect it and keep the presses of the publisher busy in supplying it. If it is not what they want, no device of type or binding or minimum cost can impose it upon them. Popular literary instincts, as popular social and political instincts, are as final in their force as they are spontaneous in their origin.

There is, therefore, such a product as light literature. Mentally, its specific gravity need not be high. Æsthetically it need not be high; and, yet, there are specific qualities of merit which it possesses that are so pronounced, that they serve to commend it to the candid attention of all writers and students of style. There is such a type as the popular style, at or below the mental and æsthetic average, and, yet, fitted to do a beneficent work where other orders of expression must fail.

We may advance a step farther and assert—that all genuine style is, to a degree, popular. The end of authorship is, that it be read, and it must exhibit, therefore, the readable or popular features. It is, in fact, one of the prime conditions of success, by the neglect or violation of which many a volume of undoubted literary and mental merit has almost immediately passed from the publisher's counters to the upper shelves of books not in demand. It is, beyond question, true that too little attention is paid by scholarly and finished writers to these popular elements of expression—to that timeliness of topics and verbal plainness and freedom of method, so essential to ensure a reading. Highly educated authors may prepare technical manuals for the schools or present scholastic papers before scholastic bodies, and rightly hold to the style of the schools, but when they enlarge their purpose and address the common public, they must endorse and exemplify those unclassified canons of style which obtain among the people and which they insist upon demanding.

We have already adduced the names of Addison and Steele, Lamb and Irving, as popular writers, in their conspicuous exhibition of these so-called taking qualities. They have been cited, also, as literary writers, and are, in a true sense, intellectual and emotive. They thus are seen to combine, in logical and beautiful unity, the four great types of style, so that it is difficult to state for which of the four they are the most notable. Prescott, our American historian, is such a popular writer, as are, also, Headley and McMaster. In biography, such names as Forster, Prior, Lockhart, Trollope, Stephen, are such writers. Such living American authors as Cable, Higginson and Warner, signally exhibit this essential unity, while in the sphere of fiction and general letters, Thackeray and Bulwer; Reade aud Kingsley, Macaulay and Hazlitt, Chesterfield, Christopher North and Charlotte Brontë conspicuously reveal it.

Holding to the intellectuality of style as its first excellence, and emphasizing, against all objections, the necessity of æsthetic beauty and of vigor, it still is incumbent on every exponent of style to present, as far as possible, his thought and his art and his passion in the form best adapted to satisfy all the normal needs of the people at large.

It is not to be accepted as tenable that a style is less scholarly because it is understood, or less artistic and effective because it is somewhat practical and pliant in its methods. All genuine mental progress and literary culture ought to be expected to evince, as one of the marks of such progress, a fuller power of adaptation to the general intellect and taste.

There is, however, another and a *lower* sense of the word popular as applied to style, and every author of high ambition is to be on his guard, at this point, against temptations to which he will be constantly exposed in his work. Popularity, at all hazards, is the creed of some writers and teachers of style. The only test of a book, they tell us, is its readableness—its salableness, irrespective of its mental or moral character. A hundred thousand copies sold means eminent merit, because it means visible success, and we are not to inquire too carefully who the hundred thousand patrons are. The books are bought and thumbed and the demand is for more. This is popularity in its lower sense, and, in this sense, we submit, there are some things better than popular success. In fact, there are few things that are worse. We have spoken of entertainment as a legitimate end of the popular style. These volumes, however, carry the idea of pleasure a trifle too far, over into the province of the illegitimate. Clearness and practical timeliness are praiseworthy features. This over-popular style, however, insists upon making matters somewhat too patent and local for the interests of truth, and what we have called picturesqueness of method degenerates into a revolting realism. There is a dirt literature, as well as a dirt philosophy, as common as dirt and as cheap as dirt and as defiling as dirt—an order of literature and of philosophy of which the modern English world has had its full supply. Popular style, as we are now viewing it, is mentally superficial, æsthetically coarse and common, and ethically impure. Marked by the absence of intellect, taste and conscience, its only object is a financial one, secured by any agency and at the expense of the best interests of the reader.

In much of our modern magazine literature, as in journalism and fiction, this is the special danger besetting our vernacular style, and specially enticing to younger writers, forming their literary habits, and anxious to record visible progress. Large and immediate dividends from small capital; the consciousness of having an ever-widening circle of readers; the satisfaction of personal pride and selfish ends; a place of prominence among the writers of the day—all this is fascinating and bewildering. Books are fast giving way to pamphlets; solid discussion to passing comment; thought and culture to more marketable qualities, and style is simply what is loosely called—"the way of putting things" so as to secure a patronage.

The attitude of the scholar and high-minded reader to all this order of expression is manifest, at once,—that of earnest protest and rebuke, the emphatic avowal of the primacy of the mental and artistic and healthfully emotional over the merely popular, even in its best forms, and, above all, a protest that, in its lower sense and function, it can have no place whatever in the purpose of the ingenuous author. Style takes its character from the thought behind it, the object before it and the measure of culture evinced therein. The first thing in writing is to have something to say worth saying, and the next best thing is to have a worthy purpose to accomplish by its utterance. Add to these conditions, the elements of literary taste, of genuine feeling, and those popular qualities of clearness and practical vigor and freedom of procedure, in so far as legitimate, and the result is an ideal English style. If, then, it is not received and read, so much the worse for the mental ability and literary judgment of the reading public, who are thereby proved, of a truth, to be in urgent need of intellectual and æsthetic training.

Upon our institutions of learning, therefore, rests, at this moment, a special responsibility, in resisting the rapid increase of an order of style and literary work which is as superficial as it is unwholesome, and which, if allowed to gain much greater dominance among us, must permanently degrade our national spirit and authorship. Written expression is the expression of thought in forms of taste and fervor and for ennobling ends, and takes its place among all the highest types of our finite, human activity. The writer is a dispenser of truth to men in methods best suited to their understandings, tastes, and rational pleasures. Better to have written a score of pages after the high Baconian method, or after the cultured model of Whipple and Lowell, or in the laudable, popular style of Howitt and Holmes, Addison and Irving, than a score of volumes in the shallow and flippant manner of the modern school of penny-a-liners in prose and verse. Better no literature whatever than an unmeaning and an unwholesome literature, bent on public applause at any price.

Despite occasional recessions and positive violations of literary laws, English and American Letters have never forgotten the exalted standards established by the earlier and later masters of style. Especially in the rich department of English prose, not a few authors, in England and at home, are engaged, at present, in friendly rivalry to maintain the character of the trust bequeathed to them. A partial reaction from the superficial and uncultured is even now apparent, and a more decided presence of the stable and artistic and vigorous elements of style. The healthful influence of Emerson and Irving; of Arnold and Whipple; of Stedman and Lowell, is widely potent among us, while in our Americen colleges themselves, the accepted centres of intellect and culture, there is the evident promise of a more intelligent and profound interest in all that pertains to American Letters and a laudable ambition to present, as writers, an order of expression alike intellectual, literary, impassioned and popular—a style that lies "four square" to all success in letters, and manifests therein the unity of truth in all its varied relations to the human mind.

THE POPULAR STYLE.

Examples.

Under that broad beech tree I sat down, when I was last this way a fishing, and the birds in the adjoining groves seemed to have a friendly contention with an echo, whose dead voice seemed to live in a hollow tree, near to the brow of that primrose hill. There I sat viewing the silver streams glide silently towards their centre, the tempestuous sea; yet, somctimes, opposed by rugged roots and pebble stones, which broke their waves and turned them with foam. . . . .

As I left this place and entered into the next field, a second pleasure entertained me. It was a handsome milk-maid, that had not yet attained so much age and wisdom as to load her mind with any fears of many things that will never be, as too many men too often do; but she cast away all care and sung like a nightingale. Her voice was good and the ditty fitted for it. It was that smooth song which was made by Kit Marlowe, now at least fifty years ago, and the milk-maid's mother sang an answer to it, which was made by Sir Walter Raleigh, in his younger days. They were old-fashioned poetry, but choicely good; I think much better than the strong lines that are now in fashion.—*Izaak Walton's "Complete Angler."*

There are but few men who are not ambitious of distinguishing themselves in the nation or country where they live, and of growing considerable among those with whom they converse. There is a kind of grandeur and respect which the meanest and most insignificant part of mankind endeavor to procure in the little circle of their friends and acquaintance. The poorest mechanic, nay, the man who lives upon common alms, gets him his set of admirers and delights in that superiority which he enjoys over those who are in some respects beneath him. This ambition, which is natural to the soul of man, might, methinks, receive a very happy turn and, if it were rightly directed, contribute as much to a person's advantage as it generally does to his uneasiness and disquiet.—*Addison's "Spectator" Papers.*

They were old chimes, trust me. Centuries ago, these Bells had been baptized by bishops; so many centuries ago, that the register of their baptism was lost long, long before the memory of man and no one knew their names. They had had their Godfathers and Godmothers, these Bells, (for my own part, by the way, I would rather incur the responsibility of being Godfather to a Bell than a Boy) and had had their silver mugs, no doubt, besides. But Time had mowed down their sponsors, and Henry the Eighth had melted down their mugs, and they now hung, nameless and mugless, in the church-tower.—*Dickens' "Christmas Stories."*

The breeze had been fresh all day, with more sea than usual, and they had made great progress. At sunset, they had stood again to the west and were ploughing the waves at a rapid rate, the Pintla keeping the head, from her superior sailing. The greatest animation prevailed throughout the ships; not an eye was closed that night. As the evening darkened, Columbus took his station on the top of the castle or cabin, ranging his eye along the dusky horizon, and maintaining an intense and unremitting watch. About ten o'clock he thought he beheld a light of glimmering at a great distance. Fearing his eager hopes might deceive him, he called to Pedro Gutienez, gentleman of the king's bedchamber, and inquired whether he saw such a light; the latter replied in the affirmative. Doubtful whether it might not yet be some delusion of the fancy, Columbus called Rodrigo Sanchez and made the same inquiry. By the time the later had ascended the round-house, the light had disappeared.—*Irving's "Columbus."*

CHAPTER V.

STYLE AND CRITICISM.

(*The Critical Style.*)

It is quite aside from the purpose of this discussion to compass the comprehensive province of general criticism. This has been done, or, at least, attempted, by no less a personage than Matthew Arnold; as he boldly declares: "I am bound by my own definition of criticism—a disinterested endeavor to learn and propagate the best that is known and thought in the world." This, we note, is a definition covering not only the ever-widening area of criticism itself, but a vast deal of territory beyond its legitimate domain.

We speak, at present, of that particular department of criticism known as literary, wherein the method and subject-matter alike are specifically those of literature, as distinct from science, philosophy, or from language itself in its purely linguistic character. Despite Mr. Arnold's all-embracing definition, he is so much a man of letters that most of his statements and conclusions as to the critical art have specially to do with literature, and, that, in modern European times. Nor is it too much to say, that what might be called the popular idea of criticism refers primarily to literature in some one or other of its manifold forms.

In so far as English literary criticism is concerned, its *origin* is comparatively recent. Mr. Hallam, in common with other literary historians of the earlier epochs of our authorship, calls attention to a kind of criticism and to various schools of critics existing in the age of Elizabeth and immediately succeeding eras. Hence, the names of Gascoigne, Webbe, Puttenham, and Sidney are enumerated, and reference is made to the metaphysical school of Donne as a critical school in the sphere of verse. Later in the history, scores of so-called-critics appear, who at the hands of some well-disposed historians receive more than a passing notice, while at the opening of the reign of Anne, and throughout the period of the classical school of letters, English literary criticism may be said to have taken on, for the first time, something like a specific and systematic form in the pages of Pope and Dryden, Addison and Samuel Johnson. Special critical treatises upon varied literary subjects were prepared and published. Such were Lord Kames' "Elements of Criticism," Burke's "Essay on the Sublime and Beautiful," Pope's "Essay on Criticism," Thomas Warton's "History of English Poetry," Alison's "Essay on Taste" and

Dr. Blair's "University Lectures on Belles Lettres" —each of these numerous discussions calling emphatic attention to the criticism of authorship as a distinctive department of scholarly effort. It is not to be forgotten that it was in the middle and latter part of this eighteenth century that the literary influence of Germany was especially felt in England, through the writings of Lessing, Herder, Schiller, and Göethe. Hence, we cannot be at a loss to account, on the one hand, for that general mental awakening of which the British mind at once became the subject, nor, on the other hand, for that distinctively critical impetus that was imparted to our national letters.

Just here we are prepared, therefore, for what may be regarded as the exact historical origin of modern English literary criticism—the establishment of the "Edinburgh Review," in 1802, in the persons of Jeffrey and his colleagues. The "Review" was pre-eminently critical and always in the definite realm of literary work. It was characteristically a review—its object being to take a scholarly survey of the authorship of the time, and pronounce judgment upon it in the light of critical canons as then established. From this date on, such a type of criticism has grown to imposing proportions, keeping even pace with the rapid development of modern English letters, and threatening, at times, to distance its natural competitor, and become an end unto itself. The name of our nineteenth century critics has already become legion, from Gifford, Lamb, Hazlitt, De Quincey, Hallam, and North on to the masterly work of Carlyle and Arnold. Such a conspicuous history of literary art as this cannot be too carefully marked by the literary student. Its characteristic features cannot be too definitely traced and all that is false be sharply distinguished from all that is true.

With the literature of England, and the style of English writers specially in view, it will be our purpose to discuss and emphasize the *essential elements* of literary criticism which, being absent, nullify or vitiate its rightful influence, but which, if effectively present, make such criticism one of the most potent factors in the literary development of a people.

I. It is needless to state, at the outset, that the presence of *general intelligence* in the person of the critic is postulated. Common information on common topics of intellectual interest is assumed. Such an one must, in a well-understood sense, be conversant, with what Mr. Arnold is pleased to phrase "the best that is known and thought in the world." He must, in Baconian speech, be a "full man," so as not "to need to have much cunning to seem to know that he doth not." If, as we are told, criticism means, to all intents and purposes, the "criticism of life," and Mr. Whipple is right in connecting literature and life, then must the critical work of every literary artist evince such an order and such a measure of the knowledge of things in general. It is to this very point that Mr. Arnold is speaking in defence of his comprehensive theory, as he says, "Judging is often spoken of as the critic's one business, but the judgment which forms itself along with fresh knowledge is the valuable one." Here the need is emphasized, on the critic's part, of an acquaintanceship with the general area and outlook of things, as if he should aim to be a kind of scholar at large, roaming at will over the vast domain of universal truth. In this respect, Leibnitz and Voltaire must have approximately answered the demands of the English essayist.

A question of more than common interest emerges just here. It refers to the necessity of what is termed a liberal education to the fulfilment of the functions of the criticism of style and letters. *A priori*, this would seem to be a tenable position. In the light of the history of criticism itself, it receives large endorsement, while, conversely, the exceptions are numerous and valid enough to keep the question still at issue.

This much, however, is to be affirmed and maintained, that a good degree of general knowledge, in whatsoever way obtained, is essential. Whether in the regular courses of academic study or in some exceptional manner, the "mental stuff," as Bacon terms it, must be possessed, as affording a valid basis, for anything like large-minded and liberal judgment. Though the acquisitions need not be encyclopedic, as were those of Leibnitz, they are to be, in the best sense, comprehensive.

We are speaking, however, of an order of knowledge specifically *literary*, a knowledge of books, and, most of all, of those books whose content, method, style and object are literary as distinct from any other possible character. Literary criticism must be based on a familiarity with literature and style as a separate province of human thought and effort. Such a critic must be a specialist in letters, as the scientific or philological critic must be in his distinct department. Whatever his scholarly attainments may be in this or that branch of learning, or however broad his knowledge may be of men and things, he must be a *littérateur*—a man of letters in the highest meaning of that term.

The few great critics of the world in the sphere of literature have been such men—pre-eminently what our First English speech calls, Bôc-Men—men of books. Such were Aristotle and Quintilian, of ancient times. Such were the Schlegels, of Germany and the wide-minded Göethe, and such, Doctor Johnson and De Quincey, of England. It is specifically of this literary knowledge that Addison is speaking in one of his critical papers as so essential to all adequate judgment. "The truth of it is," he writes, "there is nothing more absurd than for a man to set up for a critic without a good insight into all the parts of learning." His reference, throughout, is to that particular kind of learning which comes from an absorbing intimacy with classical letters. Attention has already been called to the fact that we are living in a day of critical activity. Another fact of equal importance is that ignorant criticism in the qualified sense of literary ignorance is by far too common. Even where much of our modern censorship is competent on the side of general information, it is palpably deficient in the narrower domain of literary art. The fundamental facts of literary history as a definite branch of history are not sufficiently in possession. As to the manifold relations of such history to that which is purely civil or ecclesiastical, and as to the vital relations of authors to the times in which they live and write, there is too often a manifest lack of knowledge. An accurate acquaintance with all that is meant by Taine in his frequent reference to epoch and environment as affecting literature is not sufficiently conspicuous.

It is this class of critics whom Addison designates "illiterate smatterers." They are the novices and unthinking adventurers in a sphere whose special requirements they are either unwilling to meet or incapable of appreciating. The art of criticism they regard as, at best, a kind of mechanical survey of what purports to be original with authors, and a duty, if duty at all, to be dismissed with as little thoughtfulness and preparation as possible. Modern journalism and the lighter magazine literature of the time open an attractive field in which these experimenters may ply their daily trade.

Literary criticism must, therefore, first of all, be

competent, an intelligent criticism on the literary side demanding special measures of intelligence with reference to every separate subject presented for examination. Professor Masson, in his study of Milton; and Professor Child, in his study of Chaucer and Middle English ballads, are notable examples of those who in this respect have worthily fulfilled their mission.

Such an order of criticism is as beneficent in its results as it is unyielding in its requirements. It is stimulating and suggestive to all who come under its influence. It gives what Cardinal Newman would call, "a note of dignity" to the entire province of judicial function in letters. As literature widens, it also assumes still broader forms, until, at length, the desired result is secured, that criticism becomes an important part of literature itself, and heartily co-operates therewith toward every worthiest end.

II. In the face of popular opinion to the contrary, the human *heart*, as well as the head, has something to do in the field of critical endeavor, while it is in the currency and weight of this erroneous sentiment that the need of giving due emphasis to this principle of *sympathy* or considerateness is apparent. The very words—critic, critical, and criticism—have become and still are synonymous with personal indifference; if not, indeed, with positive hostility of feeling and opinion. Mr. Gosse suggestively terms it, " executive severity." The judicial censor of books and writers is rather expected to play the part of an executioner, to have nothing to do with what Mr. Disraeli styles, the amenities. To criticise is, of course, to impale the author on the point of the critic's pen, to magnify faults and overlook excellences.

Volumes might, indeed, be written on unsympathetic criticism without going beyond the bounds of our own literature. In the days of the English bards and Scotch reviewers, it was sufficiently conspicuous. It was just here that the "Dunciad" overreached itself, and in its aim at the humorous, entered the province of the captious and cynical. It is here that the formal and fastidious school of classical poetry in the age of Dryden sadly erred, that the imperious Dr. Johnson violated the dictates of propriety, and that such a gifted man as Carlyle vitiated much of his rightful literary influence. What a sorry picture does Poe afford us in his personal vituperation of the authors of his time, who in many particulars were his superiors! What a lack of literary courtesy and good-will appears in the haughty depreciation of American poets by the infallible Whitman! Benedix, in Germany, and Voltaire, in France, were such critical cynics in their respective judgments of Shakespeare: nor is Taine, with all his merit, without deserved rebuke in this particular sphere of hypercriticism.

If we inquire more specifically as to what is meant by this element, we remark, a kindly regard for the feelings, the circumstances, and the purpose of the author under review. Mr. Arnold would call it, "urbanity." "A critic," writes Mr. Stedman, "must accept what is best in a poet and thus become his best encourager," a principle, we may add, as intrinsically true as it is finely illustrated in the author of it. Of all men, the literary critic should be a man of a humane temper of mind, full of a genuine fellow-feeling for those whose intellectual work he is called to examine. It is his duty to take as charitable and catholic a view of authors and authorship as possible, based on a wide survey of those peculiar difficulties that lie along the line of anything like original work in letters.

Here we come in contact with a distinct literary principle closely applying to the subject in hand. It maintains that, for the best results in this department of criticism, the critic and the author must be one, confirming thus the couplet of Pope:

> "Let such teach others who themselves excel,
> And censure freely who have written well."

The mere critic, in the technical sense of the word, is the least fitted to sit as a censor in any province of original production, and, most especially, in that of literature, where the most delicate phases of personal character appear, and where words are so influential over sensitive natures.

In the literature of our vernacular it is suggestive to note the large number of critics who have reached their eminence through individual authorship. One has but to run down the long list of those gifted writers who have in hand the "English Men of Letters Series" to see such a combination of style and criticism most happily exemplified. In such men as Morrison and Masson, Shairp and Hutton, Patterson and Ward, Ainger and Trollope, it would be difficult to say which was the more prominent—their critical acumen or their actual productive power as writers. If we extend this principle to the authors themselves, who are the subjects of criticism, such as Addison, De Quincey, Coleridge, and others, the result is equally striking. Of the nine American poets discussed by Mr. Stedman, the same principle is apparent in the critical work of Lowell and Taylor, much of the secret of whose power is found in the fact of their genial sweetness of temper as induced by a personal knowledge of the author's trials and discouragements. The temptation to unfeeling criticism is far too potent to be ignored. When most stoutly resisted, it will still be present with sufficient efficacy. If once allowed to control the method and spirit of critical work, it will, in the end, but defeat the very purpose of such work, and magnify the personal element above the great interests of literary art. Criticism is one thing, censoriousness is another. Keats and Henry Kirke White are not the only poets who will rise up in judgment against heartless reviewers.

It may be emphasized here that the ever-recurring errors of opinion among the wisest critics should be enough to induce in all who are called to such duty a spirit of humility and charity. It is well known in what comparative disesteem England's greatest dramatic poet was held in the seventeenth century, while scores of second-rate versifiers were lauded beyond all claims of merit. Later in our history, Edmund Waller was pronounced "the most celebrated lyric poet that England ever produced." Thomas Warton goes out of his way to compliment Hammond, and Burns must content himself with ploughing and gauging. The mere recital of England's poet laureates from 1660 on to the time of Southey is enough to awaken within us the serio-comic sentiment. Dryden excepted, the roll of honor reads as follows: Davenant, Shadwell, Tate, Rowe, Eusden, Cibber, Walton, Whitehead, and Pye, and these were the masters of literature for a century and a half after the Restoration! Fortunately for our national honor, the list opens with the name of Spencer and closes with that of Tennyson.

Critics apart, however, criticism itself as a literaary art must have something of "the milk of human kindness" in it. Even Carlyle, in his essay on Burns, goes so far as to say: "Criticism, it is sometimes thought, should be a cold business. We are not so sure of this," while in the very essay referred to the captious fault-finder forgets awhile his prevailing methods and is full of benignity. How genial as a literary judge is the kindly

Charles Lamb, as he discusses the productions of our earlier English dramatists! Sidney Smith, Christopher North, and the brothers Hare are eminent here, while one of the most attractive elements in that masterly treatise on English Letters now preparing by Henry Morley is that urbanity of temper under whose subduing influence all the rough edges of the critic's work are made to disappear.

Nor are we contending here, as we shall see hereafter, for any such thing as laxity of judgment or a sentimental deference to the character, work, and opinions of authors coming under judicial inspection. We simply maintain with Pope, that the critic and the man are one, that any order of literary judgment which separates itself from the reach and play of human sympathies is thereby devoid of one of the prime conditions of all true literary decision. Diogenes the cynic has no function in such a sphere. That truly cosmopolitan spirit, so germane to every man of letters, would forever exclude him. It is refreshing to hear the genial Richter, in speaking of Madame de Staël's "Allemagne," declare—"What chiefly exalts her to be our critic is the feeling she manifests." Richter himself was a notable example of such kindliness of spirit, adjusting all differences, subduing all enmity, and, while defending the highest canons of literary art, still applying them with suavity and grace. There is a criticism that disarms criticism. There is such a thing as the humanities in the world of letters, and no man can afford, either for his own sake or for that of literature itself, to take the censor's chair and issue his decisions in any other attitude of mind than that of considerate deference to the feelings of men.

III. Knowledge and sympathy are one thing and essential in their place. *Insight* is quite another thing, and in its place even more essential. It is what Mr. Arnold terms "the endeavor to see the object as in itself it really is." The work of the critic is now introspective and subjective, having to do with the innermost content and spirit of whatsoever may be examined.

1. There is in this included, first of all, that particular order of insight which we may call *philosophic*. As such, it has primarily to do with the fundamental laws of things, with the genesis of causes and the gradual sequence of effects. It is this phase of critical activity which the ablest critics of all ages have magnified. It is the criticism of ideas, of the essential properties of any mental product, quite apart from any specifically external form which it may assume. Even Pope, despite his slavish subjection to the formalities of Augustan art in letters, insists upon this interior insight as one of the prime conditions in those "born to judge." Criticism at this point may rise to the dignity of a philosophic science. All that is meant by the high mental process of generalization, of analysis and synthesis, is practically

involved in it. Hence, the increasingly high conception which modern educated opinion is holding as to its character and requirements. More and more, is it seen to be something more than a verbal study of authorship, and is taking its place as a substantial art, based on logical and psychological grounds.

Nothing more surely confirms this statement than the tendency manifest of late to make the boundary line between literary criticism and creation as narrow as possible. Principal Shairp, in his "Aspects of Poetry," dwells on this very subject with characteristic interest. Mr. Carlyle, in all his writings, insists upon the necessity of the inventive as well as the historical element in criticism. Precisely so, Mr. Arnold; while the latest deliverance on this particular topic is from Mr. Stedman; as he quaintly expresses it: "I doubt if creative criticism, and that which is truly critical, differ like the experimental and the analytic chemistries." In plain English, he would say, the difference is incidental and not radical. When he says of Mr. Lowell, "that to read him enjoyably is a point in evidence of a liberal education," he is speaking of his critical ability. There is, indeed, such a thing as the "higher criticism" applied to the products of literary art. It is distinctively intellectual in cast and method, so that its normal result will be seen in the form of mental quickening and expansion. It has to do far more with what De Quincey calls the "Literature of Power," than with the

"Literature of Knowledge." The one is inquisitive; the other, merely acquisitive. The judicial faculty, in whatever sphere applied, is one of the highest organs of mental energy, and reaches its conclusions largely through the agency of philosophic insight.

There is, however, a further form of insight absolutely essential to the criticism of literature. We may call it *literary*, as distinct from philosophic. Addison speaks of it as "fine taste," born with us, if at all existing, and so essential as by its absence to render all judgments fallacious. We sometimes speak of it correctly as, delicacy of perception, that peculiar reach and nicety of discrimination by which the mind comes at once to the clear discernment of what is true and beautiful in authorship. While less distinctively logical than that order of insight already noted, it is even more penetrating and crucial, and, withal, more reliable in its decisions. Unrestricted by any of the formulæ of the schools, and quite devoid of what may be called a systematic procedure, it works with all the spontaneity of instinct, and yet with all the satisfactoriness of established law. It is this that Mr. Arnold may have in mind in one of his favorite words—"lucidity." It is undoubtedly what he means by his reiterated phrase, "a sense of beauty." This is substantially what we mean by literary insight, including in its range of vision not only beauty, but all the other and higher qualities of expression. We prefer to call it, the literary sense,—founded, indeed, on literary knowledge and philosophic insight, and yet possessed of a character and territory of its own and signally exhibited in what we have discussed as, the literary style. This is that special penetration that detects, appreciates, and exhibits all the most delicate features of literary excellence in prose and verse; which peers with the genuine critic's eye, clarified by culture, into all the shades and phases of truth. It is what Hazlitt would call "the refined understanding," a sagacious apprehension of those particular qualities which make any work of art attractive and worthy. At times, as with the Greeks of old, it would seem to have been the possession of an entire people, while even in modern literature the instances are not rare when mere scholarly criticism, devoid of this unstudied perception of the inmost essence of things, has been forced to defer its literary judgments to the intuitive decisions of the general literary public. The existence of such a type and measure of insight is, however, comparatively rare, either in nations or individuals. Hence, those critics in whom this genius of criticism is found are few in number. Longinus, among the Greeks, was such an one. Such, among the Germans, was Göethe, whom Masson calls "the greatest literary critic that ever lived." Such was Sainte-Beuve in France, and such is Mr. Ruskin, of England. The very mention of these names is indicative of a keen, subtle, pervasive insight into character and art. Beyond all knowledge of fact and power of generalization there is the "vision and the faculty divine" as belonging to the critic no less than to the author. Under its searching introspection hidden things are brought to light, and truth and beauty are seen to be one.

It is pertinent to note, in this connection, that nothing is more fatal to literary progress than the presence of *superficial* literary criticism, marked alike by its lack of philosophic and of literary penetration. As already intimated, modern Continental and English Letters are showing decided progress in this particular. Since the opening of the romantic era in England, in the natural art of Burns and Wordsworth, scholars, authors, and readers alike are becoming less and less tolerant of mere verbal structure for structure's sake. Despite the fact that the conventional school of the days of Anne is far too largely reproduced by the leading poets of England, to-day, still the protest against it is so emphatic and continuous that it must perforce be heard and heeded. The gradual supremacy of substantial prose over merely resonant verse, the gradual decadence of polite letters, as the French have loosely used that phrase, and the increasing attention now given to the history, philosophy and purpose of literature, all make their influence felt within the province of criticism itself, and call for something more than mere mechanical technique. There is an ever more imperative demand among the representative classes of the community to get down below the outer body of literature to the absolute heart of things. Mr. Gosse, in his recently published criticisms—"From Shakespeare to Pope"—has, in some respects, done the literary world an important service in bringing to light undiscovered facts relative to the classical school of English letters. We confess, however, to the untimeliness of the attempt, at this late date in modern letters, to exalt beyond all proper bounds the place and work of such inferior names as Davenant and Waller, and, once again to thrust upon the notice of modern critics the methods and results of that "mundane order" of authors. The procedure is devoid of that element of insight so eminently essential to correct conclusions. If, as Mr. Gosse himself finely states it, "literature is the quintessence of good writing," and not a mere technical obedience to statute, what is needed, above all, is to encourage the tendency of modern criticism in this higher direction. If it is the "quintessence" we are seeking, then must insight both psychologic and æsthetic be applied, and the very soul of literary expression be revealed. In the absence of such insight lies the greatest deficiency of the widely versed Macaulay as a critic of letters, and, in its substantial presence, the just renown of such men as Coleridge and our American Lowell.

IV. We touch, here, upon that ever-pressing question of the precise relation of literary morality to practical and personal morals; of *ethics* to *æsthetics*. Is there such a connection as that of character and scholarship, or is the man of letters one person, and the man of ethical sensibility and aim another? The tendency of modern thinking in the domain of art and letters is undoubtedly toward an ever-widening separation of these two departments of human activity. We are told that the *littérateur* has a sphere of his own, as the moralist has his, and that nothing more is demanded of either of them in relation to the other than the observance of common civility. Such a novelist as Ouida, in her unblushing portraitures, cannot express herself too strongly against what she is pleased to call the presence of Puritanism in literature, that revolting "church steeple" authorship which is wont to express its convictions only in view of the temple and the altar. The relation of criticism to conscience becomes, in view of such deliverances as these, one of the questions of special moment. We are using the term, *conscientiousness*, in this connection, in its most comprehensive sense, as including all those elements of character that go to make up the man of honor, uprightness, and ethical integrity. Pope, in his "Essay on Criticism," especially alludes to it.

Mr. Arnold is nowhere more outspoken than just here. He protests against confining the word conscience to the moral sphere, and alludes to its exclusion from the sphere of intellectual endeavor as unscientific. The famous French critic, Sainte-

Beuve, speaks in still stronger terms. "The first consideration for us is not whether we are pleased by a work of art. What we seek above all to learn is, whether we were *right* in being pleased with it." This is certainly high ground for the Gallic mind to assume, as it at once lifts the ethical above the merely æsthetic, and gives us therein one of the fundamental elements of all literary criticism, what we style, conscientiousness. As far as the present discussion is concerned, it may be said to include three distinct essentials.

1. There must be in the critic an absolute *fidelity to the facts* as they exist. The record is to be taken as it reads, as an historical and impersonal record, as a body of data given to hand for reference and use just as it stands. The critic is not to play the legitimate *rôle* of the novelist, shaping the facts to suit his particular purpose, but must hold himself in honor bound to the facts, regarding any substantial departure therefrom as a breach of literary trust. Whatever liberty may rightfully be accorded him in the special work of the interpretation of facts, the facts themselves must stand as they are. It is here that the wide departments of literary history and biography take on a new importance as related to literary criticism, in that they serve to furnish the data obtainable from no other sources, whereby literary work itself may be the more correctly judged.

2. Into the next essential, that of *impartiality*, enters the quality of courage, an undaunted esti-

mate of merit and demerit as they stand revealed to the critic's discerning eye. Dr. Johnson's biographer has this in mind as he says, "Whoever thinks for himself and says plainly what he thinks, has some merit as a critic." We may term it, disinterestedness, a dispassionate, judicial regard to the thing in itself as quite unconnected with any ulterior end that might be subserved by it. Mr. Arnold would probably call it, justness of spirit. When Mr. Stedman speaks of Lowell as "a safe and independent critic," he must refer to this impartial attitude of mind. Mr. Froude, in his honest statements concerning Carlyle, is a good example of this heroic order of critic, while Carlyle himself, though often erring on the side of undue severity, must be classed among those few men of letters who have had the courage of their convictions and been bold to announce them in the face of all opposition.

Nor is there any necessary conflict here between what we have called literary sympathy and literary courage of decision. The tenderest deference to the feelings of authors and the fullest appreciation of their discouragements may have proper place, and yet the high demands of literary justice be fully met. If, in some exceptional emergency an apparent conflict arises and a sacrifice must be made at some point along the line, there can be no question whatever but that an inflexible justice should prevail and conscience remain supreme over the affections. Nothing is more needed in modern literature than this unbiased order of judgment, a positiveness of opinion and expression that leaves no room for debate. The very word criticism means decision. It is more than a mere discernment of truth and error, correctness and incorrectness. It is the specific deliverance of a conclusion without hesitation or evasion. Much of the practical helpfulness of criticism is found in such a fearless and final verdict as this. It tells us where we are, and affords us a basis for further procedure on intelligent methods. Better by far to err on the side of dogmatism with such open-faced censors as Arnold and Carlyle, than on the side of vacillating timidity with so many of the time-serving flatterers of the day. Pride of opinion, so it be candid and honest, is far more commendable in criticism than a craven deference to the supposed preferences of others. The surrender of one's personality is as unliterary and uncritical as it is unconscientious.

3. Conscientiousness in criticism assumes its most distinctive character as an *ethical* quality, an essential quality of high, moral aim. By this is meant, in general, a controlling regard to the demands of truth as truth. In the special department of literary criticism it means that, above all possible considerations of personal advantage, or the advantage of authors themselves, the great interests of literature should be uppermost. What will best subserve its deepening and broadening; what will purify and elevate its tone, and give it wider usefulness as a national educator; how, in fine, it

can be made what it ought to be, an essential factor in all intellectual and social progress—these are questions with which the conscientious critic is bound to deal, lest, indeed, the very end of his art be missed. The final purpose of literary criticism is what Lessing would have styled, the search after truth, first of all, as expressed in literature itself, and, then, through it as a medium in all related domains of thought. Such a purpose is eminently ethical, and serves to co-ordinate the work of the critic with that of the educator and moralist.

It is in this particular province of criticism that danger is the most imminent. Manifestly so in Continental Europe, and, most especially, in the modern French school of art, it is far too apparent on the English side of the channel, and is even working its way across the Atlantic. Mr. Gibbon has sinned as critic just here, as has Mr. Buckle, in his survey of European civilization. Mallock and Lecky are not without faults in this repect, while even such critics as John Morley and Leslie Stephen have more than once yielded to the growing tendency whereby the pursuit of truth for truth's sake has been made the secondary end. In most of the recent estimates of the character of George Eliot, it is humiliating to mark the deliberate evasion of fact and truth on behalf of a questionable morality in a woman of letters, nor is it at all possible to see just what can be gained by that exorbitant and unjustifiable laudation of the school of Whitman which at present is so prevalent among us.

Accuracy, impartiality, and moral aim positively forbid it. It is, in every true sense, unconscientious.

We speak and speak rightly of the superiority of that criticism which is constructive over that which is simply destructive and negative, while it is pertinent to emphasize the principle, just here that such an order of positive, progressive, and organizing criticism is possible only on the basis of a method and purpose controllingly ethical. Knowledge, sympathy, and insight are fundamental requisites, but that species of criticism that is grounded in these only, apart from the presence of moral aims as primary, is sure in the end to return upon itself and further every other interest but the interests of truth.

A question of lively moment arises as we close this discussion—to what extent American literary criticism is fulfilling or aiming to fulfil these essential conditions. It is this very question that Mr. Stedman seems to have in mind as he writes in the opening chapter of his "American Poets:"

> "There is little doubt that our poetry has suffered from the lack of those high and exquisite standards of criticism which have been established in older lands. Only of late have we begun to look for criticism which applies both knowledge and self-knowledge to the test, which enters into the soul and purpose of a work and considers every factor that makes it what it is. Such criticism is now essayed, but often too much occupied with foreign subjects to search out and foster what is of worth among ourselves."

The favorite theory of recent English critics that all genuine creative epochs in literature must be preceded by critical eras would seem to be having a partial illustration in the present status of our native authorship. The purely inventive era of Bryant and Longfellow, and even of Holmes and Lowell, may be said to have given way to the existing era of criticism, while it in turn is preparing the way for that highly original period of American prose and verse to which the most sanguine among us are confidently looking. Be this as it may, as in England, so at home, the present drift is rather toward the reflective examination of literary product already at hand than toward the awakening of every energy to the increasing of such product. While it is still held by some who have a right to be heard that, even yet, the main business of our American writers is to develop the national literature along the highest lines of its possible progress, there is in the country such a substantial amount of accomplished literary work as the basis of artistic criticism that such criticism will accept its opportunity and specially emphasize the questions of method, form, and external feature. For so young a people as the Americans are, and so necessarily devoted hitherto to the establishment of political and industrial life, not a little of worthy work has been done in this direction, and worthier results are promised. It is too true, indeed, that untutored and conscienceless novices insist upon experimenting within the sacred precincts of this high calling, and that American secular journalism offers too tempting a sphere for superficial and cynical judgments of men and authors. Despite this, however, it is pleasing to note that since the critical prose of Taylor and Lowell has established by example the necessity of those essentials we have aimed to discuss, there has been a more honest desire to illustrate in criticism these same essentials of knowledge, sympathy, insight, and conscience. With such names before us as Ticknor and Tuckerman, Fields and Channing, Reed and White, this hopeful spirit may find encouragement. If to this list we add those American authors who as editors of the "American Men of Letters" series, and "American Statesmen" series, may be said to be doing a high form of specifically critical work, the hopefulness is increased, while two such able critics as Mr. Whipple and Mr. Stedman are enough in themselves to inspire confidence as to our future.

Nor must the liberal institutions of the land be omitted in this general estimate. Their distinctive title is that of *literary* institutions. Whatever their defects have been as to high literary tone and critical competency, it is more and more apparent that in these particulars worthier views are obtaining and the colleges of the country are fast becoming accepted standards of literary judgment. The question propounded of late, whether a national academy of letters would be best in America, is, after all, subordinate, to the further question, as to the possibility of founding numerous centres of literary influence among us. As Mr. Howells recently suggests, what is needed in America is not that this or that city should be an acknowledged primate in the Republic of American authorship, but that we have "a literary centre scattered all over the country in keeping thus with the spirit of federal nationality." There is here, we submit, a possible result open to our liberal institutions, in the realization of which all that has hitherto been done will appear insignificant. If we need and are to have in this country an order of criticism worthy of the name, then must our literary schools of learning become indeed literary, the sources of continuous literary product, the accepted centres the country over of all that is worthy in æsthetic art and culture.

We are full of hope in this particular. American letters are to become a substantial power in the land. Literary progress is to rank among us as second to no other form of progress. The colleges of our future are to be as never before the homes of high taste. Criticism is to mean, most especially literary criticism, the criticism of style and authorship, while from these multiplied seats of literary activity, as of scientific and philosophic, there will ever go forth an influence so potent and pervasive that the remotest frontiers of our national domain will feel it. Perchance, the American greed for gold and civic preferment will, under such an influence, give way at length to an equally intense and expressive passion for generous and lofty culture.

This in itself will make our literature and our criticism competent, catholic, discriminating, and conscientious. It will, also, serve to place us as a people fairly in line with our "kin beyond the sea," who, even yet, with all their decline from earlier standards, continue to hold among the nations of modern times the enviable place of literary leadership.

THE CRITICAL STYLE.

Examples.

If ever any author deserved the name of an original, it was Shakespeare. Homer himself drew not his art so immediately from the fountains of nature; it proceeded through Egyptian channels. The poetry of Shakespeare was inspiration indeed; he is not so much an imitator as an instrument of nature; and 'tis not so just to say that he speaks from her as she speaks through him. His characters are so much nature, herself, that 'tis a sort of injury to call them by so distant a name as copies of her.—*Pope's Preface to "Tonson's Shakespeare."*

In Milton's mind itself there were purity and piety absolute; an imagination to which neither the past nor the present were interesting except as far as they called forth and enlivened the great idea in which and for which he lived; a keen love of truth which, after many weary pursuits, found a harbor in the sublime listening to the still small voice in his own spirit and a keen love of his country which expanded into a love of man. These alone could be the conditions under which such a work as Paradise Lost could be conceived and accomplished.—*Coleridge's "Literary Remains."*

I know not whether I have been so careful of the plot and language as I ought; but, for the latter, I have endeavored to write English as near as I could distinguish it from the tongue of pedants. Only I am sorry that we have not a more certain measure of it, as they have in France. I wish we might at length cease to borrow words from other nations which is now a wantonness in us, not a necessity. But I fear, lest, defending the received words, I shall be accused of following the new way, I mean, of writing scenes in verse. Though, to speak properly, it is not so much a new way amongst us, as an old way new revived; for, many years before Shakespeare's plays, was the tragedy of Queen Gorboduc in English verse.—*Dryden's Dedication to the "Rival Ladies."*

It is an open question, however, whether a poet need be conscious of the existence and being of the laws and conditions under which he produces his work. It may be a curb and detriment to his genius that he should trouble himself about them in the least. But this rests upon the character of his intellect and includes a further question of the effects of culture. Just here there is a difference between poetry and the cognate arts of expression, since the former has somewhat less to do with material processes and effects. The freedom of the minor sculptor's, painter's or composer's genius is not checked, while its scope and precision are increased, by knowledge of the rules of his calling and of their application in different regions and times. But in the case of the minor poet, excessive culture and wide acquaintance with methods and masterpieces, often destroy spontaneity.—*Stedman's "Victorian Poets."*

CHAPTER VI.

PROSE STYLE AND POETRY.

(*The Poetic Style.*)

ONE of the most interesting and instructive studies in style and general literature is, what may be termed, the relation of literary forms,—that of the oral form of open address to the written form of the essay or article ; that of the didactic to the argumentative; that, especially, of prose to poetry.

There is in existing authorship, indeed, so large a border-ground between specific poetical and prose expression that the department of what the critics call, poetical prose, is one that is demanding and receiving an ever-increasing attention. It is that species of prose which, not being metrical, cannot, in any valid sense, be called verse, and, yet, which is possessed of such an unusual degree of rhythm or verse quality that it departs materially from prose proper and becomes a kind of separate or intervening form—having its own distinctive character, attraction and purpose. Such is much of Hawthorne's prose-fiction, as expressed in such works as, "The Scarlet Letter" and "The Marble Faun." Indeed, so prevalent is this poetical quality in the novel as a specific class of literature, that the question is still an open one, whether fiction more accurately belongs to the realm of prose or verse, so able a writer as Moir contending with Minto and others for its classification with the latter. Minto deliberately excludes Fiction from his discussion of prose literature. Even so acute a critic as Masson divides literature so as to bring the Novel under Poetry; as he states, "The Novel, at its highest, is a Prose Epic."

This discussion apart, however, the high poetic quality of much of our best English Prose still remains and marks it as belonging to a transitional era. No more striking example of this order of prose can be found than some of the productions of Mr. Swinburne, as his "Victor Hugo," "Study of Shakespeare," and "Miscellaneous Essays," it being especially noticeable here, that this very prose which is so poetical is *critical* prose, in which we would expect to find the least possible expression of the verse quality.

So, at the other extreme, we note an order of poetry that may be called—Prose Poetry, as illustrated in much of the verse of Pope, Cowper, Thomson, Akenside, Pollock, Rogers and Tupper —a type of verse that is so didactic as to raise the issue, whether it is verse at all, save in the one sense of being in metrical structure.

This dependence and inter-dependence of forms can, however, best be seen through the medium of historical proof, by noting the large and illustrious list of authors who have been writers both of prose and verse—in some cases, making prose subordinate; in others, verse; and in others, still, dividing their time and talent so evenly as to make it quite impossible to say in which department they have done the better work.

Of the first class we may cite such names as, Chaucer, Spenser, Ben Jonson, Milton, Pope, Mrs. Browning, and Longfellow; of the second order, such as, Addison, Dr. Johnson, Swift, Macaulay, Coleridge, Wordsworth, Matthew Arnold, George Eliot, and Emerson; and of the third order, such names as, Dryden, Sir Walter Scott, Swinburne, Holmes, Bryant and Lowell. Such variety of literary product from our classic authors reveals, beyond question, the mutual indebtedness of one form of literature to another, and, most especially, that on which we are now insisting—the indebtedness of prose to verse.

The cases in English Letters, or, indeed, in general literature, are comparatively rare in which standard poets have written nothing but poetry, or standard prose writers nothing but prose. Examples of the first class, such as Shakespeare, Burns, Byron, Shelley, Robert Browning and Tennyson, and examples of the second order, such as, Bacon, De Quincey, Burke, Carlyle and Irving, are not sufficiently numerous as exceptions to invalidate the principle of this clearness of connection. It would be difficult, if not impossible, for such prose writers as Scott and Swinburne to state the full character and measure of their indebtedness as prose writers to poetry itself and to the reactive influence of their own poetic work. A part of such influence is discernible and measurable, but the larger part is an unconscious one and, of course, not reducible to exact estimate. If this be so, there must be qualities of style and art common to both, and, it is, therefore, our special purpose at present to discover and discuss such qualities.

Stating the idea in the form of a question, we may ask—What those qualities are, as we find them in the best prose and prose style, which have largely or mainly been secured from the domain of verse. In answering this question, we shall find it best to follow, though in a different order, the fourfold division of the representative types of style that we have already discussed, viz:—The Intellectual, Impassioned, Popular and Literary.

I. The Intellectual Element. We encounter here, at once, the open question as to whether there is, indeed, any strictly intellectual element in verse, and, if conceded to exist, whether it can be said to be sufficiently prominent to make it an essential quality, and thus to make its influence on prose style materially effective. As the subject lies before us, it must, at the outset, be acknowledged that poetry has distinctively mental features and must, therefore, to a degree exert a mental influence upon other forms of literature. There is such a thing as creative verse, what Mr. Arnold would call—the Poetry of Ideas—the specific product of original suggestion. It is inventive and indicative, rather than imitative or exhaustive—a type of poetic effort in which poetic genius finds its fullest exercise. Homer and Dante, Shakespeare and Milton, Æschylus and Racine, were such poets and have thus written, and, in so far as they have affected prose expression and general letters, have affected them on the intellectual side. Who of us could with certainty aver that such a creative author as Göethe was intellectually greater in prose than he was in verse, or fail to concede that to each of these species of authorship he brought the same genius with equally effective results!

Such an order of poetic genius, however, is historically rare—so rare, indeed, as to constitute the exception rather than the rule. We see its presence in a few epics; in a few dramatic masterpieces and, here and there, in the domain of lyric, as in Schiller and Burns. Hence, we must affirm that, while poetry is possessed of an intellectual quality and has an influence on prose along mental lines, such a quality and such an influence are so limited, as to make them comparatively indirect and incidental, and we must look elsewhere for the dominant influence of verse over prose.

II. The Impassioned Element. Here we come within an area definitely poetic, both as to character and extent. Most of the definitions of poetry, as given by the older and later writers, not only include this emotional feature, but make it the conspicuous one. Aristotle and Longinus, Byron and Macaulay, Mill and Ruskin so represented it. This is what Shakespeare means by the "fine frenzy" of the inspired bard. Poetry is pre-eminently the language of the heart, the most natural and potent interpreter of the soul of man, his joys and sorrows, hopes and fears, loves and hates. Hence the antiquity and prevalence of lyric verse, in ode and sonnet, in elegy and pastoral,—as old as the race and as wide-reaching as the experiences of man. That distinctively spiritual element which is of the very essence of poetry is essentially emotional—the expression of the nature in its most devout and intense interior life. Hence, Poetry is an inspiration and an aspiration—a deep, all-controlling sense and an equally far-reaching outlook into the infinite and supernal.

The effect of all this upon prose and prose style is manifest at once. Simply because feeling is so natural, self-expressive and unconfined in its range, no conventional distinction between prose and poetry can suffice to check its outflow or confine it to this or that particular sphere of authorship. The impassioned poet will be the impassioned prose writer, and, even when the prose author never enters the domain of verse, his style and method will be emotive just to the degree in which he comes in contact with poetry as sensuous and fervent. No writer of prose can place himself in constant contact with such poets as Burns and Mrs. Browning, Schiller and Herder, and our American Longfellow, and not be moved to some measure of passion. No better school could be found for the cultivation of style on the side of genuine sentiment, than a personal and profound acquaintance with the leading lyrics and lyrists of the world. It would be difficult, indeed, for such an author to write prosaic prose, or to be technical, didactic and dispassionate, to any extreme degree.

Feeling is begotten by feeling, and the deepest sensibilities of our natures are awakened by such lyrists as Milton and Wordsworth, Gray and Moore, in that they sing from the heart out and only because they must. All prose writing of the highest order, as we have seen, must be, to a degree, impassioned, in order to be effective, and such a quality is due, in no small measure, to the natural influence of verse.

III. The Popular Element. Next to fiction and descriptive miscellany, poetry is probably the most widely diffused and widely read form of modern literature, partly, by reason of its metrical structure; partly, because of the wide variety of its topics in epic, drama and lyric; partly, because of the flexibility and freeness of its method and range, but, mainly, because of its final purpose, to gratify.

Poetry is popular because it ministers to personal pleasure, its office being entertainment rather than discipline or instruction. It is so widely read because it is so thoroughly readable.

It is at this point that we meet one of the most radical differences between verse and prose, in that what is primary in the one—pleasure—is secondary in the other, and hence, the importance of emphasizing, as far as possible, any relation of helpfulness that may exist between them,—prose contributing to poetry some of its more stable and substantial qualities, while it, in turn, receives from poetry something of its lighter, more facile and attractive features. While insisting, throughout, that the didactic element is and should be the prominent one in prose style, it is still in place to press the claims of the popular element, especially in view of the growing tendency to make our prose writing too scientific, abstract and unreadable. Prose and poetry are alike in this respect—that they are written to be read, and fail of their respective purpose, in so far as they are difficult of reading. Popular prose, we submit, should not be confined to journalism, fiction and miscellany, but should have a much fuller expression than it now has in all the higher spheres of prose—in history and biography; in philosophy and criticism, and even in logical dissertation and discussion. Macaulay is none the less to be admired as an historian, nor Masson as a biographer, nor Descartes as a philosophical author, nor Lowell as a critic, because, in their respective writings, they are readable and evince the popular elements of authorship. In fact, much of their superiority in these departments of authorship to those who have written on similar topics lies in the fact that, with equal mental ability, they have been able to express it in more tangible and appreciable forms.

It is to be noted, just here, that while all poetry in its effect on prose is, to a degree, popularizing, the lighter forms of poetry, as seen in lyric and descriptive verse, are especially so, not excepting, of course, that division of dramatic art which comes under comedy. Here, therefore, as in the sphere of feeling, all the great lyrists of literature have a helpful mission to the writer of prose, as, also, the leading descriptive poets, such as Thomson and Cowper, Beattie and Campbell, Bryant and Whittier. To be thoroughly conversant with such poets as these is to see and appreciate that which makes their poetry pleasing, and thus to be incited to reproduce it to some extent within the sphere of prose. We gain thereby a freer play of power as authors, a somewhat lighter touch of hand, a flowing facility and scope of movement, whose effect upon our style will be liberative and healthful and go far to relieve it of any tendency to the uniform and unreadable. There is such a thing as *prose license,* though not so pronounced as license in verse. The writer, while substantially keeping within prescribed limits and observing the fundamental laws of prose expression, must yet be allowed and encouraged to be, at times, superior to his conditions—more unrestrained and popular, though none the less effective.

IV. The Literary Element. We are now brought to the most distinctive element of poetry, and to its most characteristic contribution to prose. It includes all that is embraced under the terms, æsthetic or artistic. It magnifies up to the fullest legitimate limit the form of verse as distinct from the subject matter, and insists that poetry, purely in its external or structural feature, has an important function to fulfil relative to all the varieties of prose expression. As the romantic school of the later Georgian era emphasized the impassioned quality of poetry, what is known as the critical or classical school of Augustan days emphasized the structure, as seen in Pope and Prior, and largely exhibited in the Modern Victorian school. In so far as Mr. Arnold has written poetry, he has done so from this point of view, and, in so far as he has given an estimate of other poets, has made his estimate dependent upon the presence or absence of this artistic feature. Keats and Gray he would rank above Byron, mainly on this principle; in that they display in a signal manner the technique of verse. Poetry, in this sense, is an art rather than an intuition or an inspiration. Verbal execution is its commanding characteristic. A poem is a something architectural—built up after a design and upon a well-defined method—and when finished, relatively faultless. The poet is an artist.

Conceding, as Mr. Arnold does, that there are other elements, mental and emotional, in verse, and conceding, as Mr. Arnold does not, that these have a larger place in verse than modern criticism allows, it is still correct to say, that if distinction is to be made, the most distinguishing feature of poetry is its metrical or structural feature, its specifically artistic form, so that whatever may be the indebtedness of prose to verse, as to intellectual, impassioned or popular qualities, its distinctive indebtedness is a literary one. While prose and poetry are alike literary, poetry is more conspicuously so than prose, and while it may be obliged to borrow certain qualities from its kindred form, it is its unquestioned prerogative to minister to the prose author that type of product that we term, æsthetic.

Some of these literary qualities thus contributed to prose style may be briefly examined.

1. Beauty and Sublimity. Of these attractive characteristics, poetry, as we know, may be said to possess an especial measure. These eliminated, and poetry itself is virtually absent. Though, as a matter of theory, whatever is metrical is, thereby, constituted verse; as a matter of historical and practical moment, that only is poetry which is poetical in its nature or subject matter. In this respect—the supremacy of the sense—poetry and prose stand on common ground, the difference being in the particular manner in which the idea is

embodied and expressed. While in prose production, beauty of external form may or may not be prominent, in poetry, such a quality is radical and vital, and, in so far as it is prominent, marks the product as poetic. There is such a thing as beauty and sublimity of structure, germane to the very idea of verse, as clearness and mental vigor are germane to standard prose.

In speaking, therefore, of the relation of indebtedness of prose to verse, it is in place to state, that the element of beauty should exist, in some measure, in all acceptable writing, and that such writing is dependent for this quality especially upon verse. The more fully they act and interact, the more fully will the æsthetic elegance of the one form pass over into the other and modify it. That ease and grace of movement which we find in such an essayist as Charles Lamb, was not due entirely to the fact that his very nature was poetic, but to his wide acquaintance with the best English verse of the time preceding him. He had so possessed himself of the meaning and inner spirit of the old English dramatists, that when he came to write prose, he wrote it with a poetic ease and naturalness, which, otherwise, he could not have evinced. This interaction is signally illustrated in those writers who have accomplished much alike in prose and verse. Whatever the effect of the prose on the verse may have been, that of the verse on the prose has been more decided and lasting. Who of us can tell how much Macaulay owed, in the line of poetic beauty, to his "Lays of Ancient Rome;" how much more pacific and graceful Milton would have been in his political writings, had he written his poetry first; how the elegance of verse would have softened and subdued the crabbed character of Carlyle as a writer, and how, as a matter of fact, it did modify the style of Addison and Dryden, Pope and Wordsworth and Coleridge!

We have, as it occurs to us, in our own American Emerson, a striking example of the benign and beautifying effect of poetry over prose. Possessed of a style naturally intellectual, philosophic and ethical rather than artistic, his prose authorship clearly evinces the æsthetic effect of his verse, until, at the close of his career as an author, when we are called upon to estimate his rank and influence as a writer, we are constrained to give the poetic feature a much larger place than was assigned it by his earlier critics. In a word, poetry *poetizes* prose. In the form of the epic and tragic drama, it imparts to it sublimity, while in the lighter forms of comedy, lyric and descriptive verse, it imparts beauty and grace. Dignity and finish of structure are alike derived. The elevating influences of such productions as the "Iliad," "Paradise Lost," "Hamlet," "The Medea" and "The Divina Commedia," combine with the classical correctness of such poems as "The Endymion" of Keats; Tennyson's "Princess;" Shelley's "Adonais" and Lowell's "Vision of Sir Launfal."

The late Matthew Arnold was never weary of calling our attention to what he styled "the genius and instinct for beauty,"—a quality of verse which his own poetry exemplifies, and a quality of prose which, in so far as it exists, is mainly derivable from verse itself. To this extent, at least, every prose author must be a poet.

2. Imagery and Figurative Force. In speaking of the office of the imagination relative to authorship, a distinction is carefully to be made between what metaphysicians call, the philosophic imagination, and that which literary critics call, the poetic. The one is especially exercised within the sphere of mental philosophy and higher discussion, while the other finds its natural province within the sphere of verse. It is to this latter, therefore, that we refer in speaking of the indebtedness of prose to poetry. While in the elevated strains of epic and tragic verse, the imagination is employed in its highest constructive and, combining work, as "the vision and faculty divine, this is rather its exceptional function. Shakespearean, Homeric and Miltonic song is not the prevailing order, so that in the expression of the vast body of poetry as a literary product,—in ode and sonnet, sketch and pastoral—it is the poetic or descriptive imagination that is called into play. The Fancy as distinct from the imagination has a function here. The work is graphic, delineative and pictorial rather than philosophic. It is the "poet's eye with a fine frenzy rolling, glancing from heaven to earth and

earth to heaven." It is the specifically discursive or excursive office of this faculty, as confined to no assigned bounds, but roaming and moving at will to the farthest ends of the earth and to the highest heights of heaven.

Here, again, our best prose authorship is much indebted to verse. Poetry is essentially imaginative and figurative, as prose is essentially unimaginative and literal. Our very word prose signifies directness—the clearest, tersest expression of the thought, and, as a theory, allows of no margin or license. Hence, the danger of undue compactness, tending to the rigid, monotonous and mechanical; and it is just here that literature on its imaginative, metrical side enters to poetize prose, to emancipate it from its restrictions; to enlarge its scope and bounds, and, while allowing it to retain its fundamental features, to insist on adding thereto something of the poetic. There is such a thing as a symbolic prose style—a picturesque method of setting forth abstract truth so that it shall reveal the idea as a painter reveals character in scenery.

Historical Portraiture is a striking example of this, as seen in Macaulay's description of the trial of Hastings; or in Presçott's description of Mexican and Peruvian life; or in Motley's recital of the trial and death of John of Barnevelde.

Fiction is full of this verbal delineation, as seen, especially, in Victor Hugo. Forensic address, as illustrated in Grattan and Burke, has notable examples of it, just enough to illustrate the possibility of its expression and just enough to show the desirability of its fuller expression. Poetry is eminently symbolic. Personal contact with it, in its best forms, will make a style symbolic. Plato cannot safely be followed, as he excludes it from his ideal republic, and we are rather to follow those illustrious prose authors, from Cicero on to Bacon and De Quincey, who, while devoting their best energies as authors to prose production, recognize, throughout, the validity of verse and its manifold ministries to the writers of prose.

3. Euphony. In such a literary quality of poetry as this, so essential to the very existence of it, we notice several characteristics, each of which is important in its place, and each of which may be said to have a helpful relation to prose. We are not speaking now, exclusively, of poetry as metrical, based on what is called, the science of versification and subject to its principles. This, of course, is involved. We include all that pertains to poetic sound—to the way in which poetry strikes the ear and appeals, through that medium, to the poetic sense within us. There is such a law as agreeableness of sounds, of sounds in themselves, as uttered in the form of vowels and liquids, and of sounds, as expressive of the meaning behind them. All that is included in melody and harmony is here designated. Alliteration, as seen in First English verse, expressed it, while alliterative usage, as even now allowable, is especially euphonic. No one word will better express what we here mean by

euphony, whether confined to poetry or transferred to prose, than rhythm. Poetry is essentially rhythmic, and it is in point to add, that the best prose and prose style should be, to an extent, rhythmic. It should be euphonic. It should sound well, pleasing the ear as well as the mind and æsthetic taste,—never, indeed, becoming, as in verse, a primary feature but, still, existent and evident and more and more so as the particular idea of the poem demands it. Edgar Allan Poe's "Bells" is the success that it is because he gave it the special euphonic element that the idea demanded. Wordsworth's "Excursion" has less and needed less. So, in prose, the euphonic element may vary, called for, in large measure, in such a production as Sidney's "Arcadia" or Johnson's "Rasselas" or Mills' "History of the Crusades," while less urgently demanded in more didactic authorship.

There is, of course, a vast natural difference here in the standard prose of different peoples. That of the Greek and Latin races is more rhythmic than that of the Teutonic. Such a language as the Italian, whether in prose or poetry, is essentially euphonic, full of vowel and liquid resonance, falling upon the ear so pleasantly as, at the time, to charm and captivate us and tempt us to forget the idea itself in its fascinating utterance. As to our vernacular English, though the South European element is large, the old Northern element is larger and more potent. English is not conspicuously musical. Its complexity forbids this, while the modern type of English character as enterprising and practical, gives prominence to the more rugged consonantal elements, at the expense of the softer vocables given it from Southern Europe. English prose needs this rhythmic element, up to the full measure of its possible expression, so long as under the control of the subject matter. The melody of Swinburne's prose writings, fascinating as it is, has perchance carried the principle of vocalism a trifle too far. In the prose authorship, however, of Masson and of Morley; of Stedman and of Lowell, we discover its more normal and healthful expression and its real indebtedness to poetry.

Suggestions.

We have thus briefly noticed the various contributions—intellectual, impassioned, popular and literary—which verse may be said to make to prose style.

Two or three suggestions of practical import are now in place.

I. The Prose Writer and the student of prose authorship and style should make himself conversant with the Principles and Laws of Poetic Expression—with poetry on its scientific side, having its well-defined basis and method. The study of such an author as Ruskin is, to this end, essential. Prof. Gummere, in his "Hand Book of Poetics," has given us valuable knowledge in this technical direction, as, also, the Poet, Lanier, in his "Structure of English Verse." The able treatises on Metre by Schipper and Ten Brinck of Germany; by Ellis, of England, and by Prof. Child, of Harvard, are in the same scientific direction. Aristotle, in his "Rhetoric" and "Poetics," thus discusses it. Longinus, among the Greeks; Göethe and Lessing, Schiller and Hegel and the brothers Schlegel, among the Germans, have developed it; while in England, from the publication of Sidney's "Defence of Poesie," on through the writings of Dryden and Wordsworth, Burke and Alison, Swinburne and Arnold, Symonds and Shairp, Dobson and Lang, Gosse and Ward, Stedman and Lowell, the whole subject of verse, on its critical side, has been fully presented for the guidance of the student. In fine, what is called, Literary Criticism, has been and is now, mainly, the criticism of poetry with reference to its own nature and its relation to other literary forms.

Care must be taken, indeed, lest a study necessarily so technical become too technical, so that the scientific be made an end in itself. This result would defeat the very purpose in view by reducing poetic science and criticism to the baldest forms of prose discussion. Poetry is a science, and yet, of all sciences, the one in which the didactic element is to be made the least conspicuous—the only object of the science being to establish guiding laws of structure and procedure by which poetry as an art may be made the more excellent and permanent.

All that is involved in the study of poetic forms properly falls under such a scientific survey,—as to the nature and conditions of the epic; as to the real relations of the tragic, comic and historical drama; as to the multiform divisions of lyric verse, in the elegy, pastoral and sonnet; as to the rank and function of didactic and general descriptive verse; as to the numerous subordinate varieties of verse, in metrical romance, metrical chronicle, the serio-comic, satire, melodrama, farce, ballad and idyll; in fact, a philosophic as well as an artistic study of poetry, whereby the outlook of the student shall be enlarged and a position be attained from which correct literary estimates may be made.

II. A further necessity to the student of style, as style relates to verse, is a thorough acquaintance with Standard Poetry. We refer now to poetry as an art—to its actual embodiment in literary product; as seen in the best specimens of native and foreign bards. It is scarcely necessary to state in detail the poets and poems that are thus to be read. Suffice it to say, that the few great epics of literature are to be mastered; that the historic masterpieces of the drama, as seen, especially, in the great Greek and English dramatists, are to be examined as works of art; and the choicest lyrics of all nations to be read and re-read. Nor is this to be merely a reading, but a study; nor merely a study, but an appreciative and all-absorbing pursuit—such a sympathetic identification of the student and poem, that the innermost spirit of the bard and of his utterance shall be caught and assimilated. It is this poetic spirit, back of all line and stanza, back of all epic and lyric, that is the one thing desirable to be gained by the student of style, if so be his work as a prose author is to reflect the influence of the verse he peruses. He must place himself, to some extent, in the mental and emotional attitude of the poet whom he reads; must forget, for the moment, all conventional distinctions between prose and verse; must become, in a sense, a poet himself and submit himself, without reserve, to the fullest influences of his author. Such a receptive spirit is essential to the best results and, if fully exhibited, will enable the writer, approximately at least, to be Homeric, Shakespearean or Tennysonian in his prose style.

Most especially, must the highest prose writer make himself conversant with the best English verse—must know it, from first to last; from Caedmon to Swinburne, as he knows his alphabet; must understand its governing thought, its vital spirit, its peculiarity of structure, its grounds of strength and merit, and must be steeped in it and inspired by it, so as to write, when he writes, with its best examples conspicuously in view, and in his most distinctive prose productions evince something of the poetic idea and passion. If poetry, as the ancients insisted, is a gift of the gods and supernatural in its character, surely no writer of prose, as the more human type of expression, should be content to be devoid of something of this divine afflatus and power.

We close with the thought, that there is, in the present stage of our literary development, special need of the poetic element in prose.

Macaulay's pronounced belief, that, as civilization advances, poetry declines, would seem to be visibly verified among us, as we note the gradual decadence of masterful verse under the growing materialism of modern times. Poets and prose writers alike must be truer than ever to the primary poetic instincts of the heart and protest, by voice and pen, against their continued suppression. The best prose of the age need be none the less able or effective by being somewhat more poetic, more impassioned, literary and popular. With all its mental vigor preserved and its characteristic qualities as prose preserved, nothing can be lost and much gained by adding grace to intellect; finish, to force; culture to correctness, and so illustrate the biblical union of "strength and beauty."

The prose writer is, first of all, a thinker, but, next to that, and closely, next, a man and an artist, possessed of a human soul and a natural taste which must find expression in form and æsthetic order. There is in all good prose what Mr. Arnold has happily called—"a sense of beauty." We may call it—the sense of form, the presence and potency of literature as an art, while it is becoming here to say that among all the beneficent ministries of the late Matthew Arnold to English Letters, none has been more pronounced or helpful, than his earnest insistence, as the self-appointed apostle of culture, upon the necessity of poetic style in English prose. No literary product, he would tell us, is worthy the high appellation of literary until it is shapely and comely in its structural form. Style, as the art of presentation, must, in the nature of things, be made presentable. Such teachings as these are eminently timely and, when more fully exemplified than now, will serve to show the true indebtedness of prose to verse and, thereby, also, show the law of literary unity.

THE POETIC STYLE.

Examples.

Waves of clear sea are, indeed, lovely to watch, but they are always coming or gone, never in a taking shape to be seen for a second. But here was one mighty wave that was always itself, and every fluted swirl of it constant as the wreathing of a shell. No wasting away of the fallen foam, no pause for gathering of power, no hopeless ebb of discouraged recoil; but alike through bright day and lulling night, the never-pausing plunge and never-fading flush and never-hushing whisper, and, while the sun was up, the ever-answering glow of unearthly aquamarine, ultramarine, violet blue, gentian blue, peacock blue, river-of-paradise blue, glass of a painted window melted in the sun and the witch of the Alps flinging the spun tresses of it forever from her snow.—*Ruskin's "Praeterita."*

My dream expanded and moved forward. I trod again the dust of Posilipo, soft as the feathers in the wings of Sleep. I emerged on Baia; I crossed her innumerable arches; I loitered in the breezy sunshine of her mole; I trusted the faithful seclusion of her caverns, the keepers of so many secrets; and I reposed on the buoyancy of her tepid sea. Then Naples and her theatres and her churches, and grottoes and dells and forts and promontories rushed forward in confusion, now among soft whispers, now among sweetest sounds, and subsided and sank and disappeared. Yet a memory seemed to come fresh from every one; each had time enough for its tale, for its pleasure, for its reflection, for its pang. As I mounted with silent steps the narrow staircase of the old palace, how distinctly did I feel against the palm of my hand the coldness of that smooth stone-work.—*Landor's "Pentameron."*

The sun was now resting his huge disk upon the edge of the level ocean and gilded the accumulation of towering clouds through which he had traveled the livelong day, and which now assembled on all sides, like misfortunes and disasters around a sinking empire and fallen monarch. Still, however, his dying splendor gave a sombre magnificence to the massive congregation of vapors, forming out of their unsubstantial gloom the show of pyramids and towers; some, touched with gold; some, with purple; some, with a hue of deep and dark red. Nearer to the beach, the tide rippled around in waves of sparkling silver, that imperceptibly, yet rapidly, gained upon the sand.—*Sir Walter Scott's "Antiquary."*

But before Mr. Dimmesdale had done speaking, a light gleamed far and wide over all the ruffled sky. It was doubtless caused by one of those meteors which the night-watcher may so often observe burning out to waste in the vacant regions of the atmosphere. So powerful was its radiance that it thoroughly illuminated the dense medium of cloud betwixt the sky and earth. The great vault brightened like the dome of an immense lamp. It showed the familiar scene of the street with the distinctness of mid-day, but, also, with the awfulness that is always imparted to familiar objects by an unaccustomed light. The wooden houses, with their jutting stones and quaint gable-peaks; the door-steps and thresholds, with the early grass springing up about them; the garden-plots, black with freshly-turned earth; the wheel-track, little worn and, even in the market-place, margined with green on either side—all were visible.—*Hawthorne's* "*Scarlet Letter.*"

CHAPTER VII.

STYLE AND SATIRE.

(The Satirical Style.)

HISTORICALLY, satire is an old Roman or Latin form, in its origin, and may be said to have had its first embodiment in the writings of Ennius, 240 B. C.–190 B. C. Still more accurately, it assumed, for the first time, its more distinctive and modern character in the works of Lucilius, 148 B. C.–103 B. C. It was Lucilius who first wrote of men and manners in that peculiar strain now common to satire, and established it on a literary basis, from which it has not materially departed. After a period of nearly half a century, the great satirist of the Augustan age arose, 65 B. C.–8 B. C., in the person of Horace, author of no less than thirty distinct satires, in addition to numerous compositions more or less satirical.

Passing over to the Christian era, 34–62 A. D., Persius appears, author of several satires, and connected, in Latin literary history, with his successor and superior, the renowned Juvenal. The date of Juvenal's birth is in doubt, but he lived, as we know, in the reigns of Nero, Domitian and Hadrian, in the latter part of the first and the opening of the second century of the Christian era. Of the sixteen satires of Juvenal and his well-deserved celebrity in this particular sphere, it is needless here to speak. Martial, the epigrammatist, born in Spain, 43 A. D., but residing at Rome, 66 A. D., is properly included in this historical sketch. Lucian, also, a great classic satirist, born at Samosata, Syria, at the opening of the second century, 130 A. D., and living till its close, is also included.

In his way and time, no author of Greece or Rome wielded a more varied pen. Whether in criticism, biography, poetry or miscellany, he was always satirical. Especially in his romance of "The Two Histories," and in his "Dialogues," such as, "The Sale of Lives;" "Dialogues of the Gods;" "Timon the Misanthrope;" "Dialogues of the Dead," and others, sarcasm and humor are so combined as to give pungency and spirit throughout.

Pietists and philosophers were the most frequent targets for the shafts of his ridicule and contempt, or, as Froude expresses it, "the abominations of paganism and the cant of the popular philosophers." He loved nothing better than to impale upon the point of his satire either some notorious theory or personage of the time, until each one saw it as he saw it. He was the Juvenal of his age and nation, a kind of compound of Swift and Voltaire, and could not have written otherwise than he did without belying the deepest instincts of his nature and surrendering to inferior authors a sphere for which he had special gifts.

Passing on beyond the fall of the Roman Empire to the closing centuries of the middle ages, two names of special note appear, in the persons of Rabelais and Erasmus. The one, in his "Pantagruel and Gargantua;" and the other, in his "Colloquia," dealt out stinging invectives against the social corruption and, most especially, the priestly vices of the time. No more pungent diatribes against "spiritual wickedness in high places" can be found in extant literature.

Coming down to the sixteenth century and to what may be termed, the revival of satire in Modern Europe, we see it, as might be expected, to a limited extent in Germany and, in its fullest expression, in France and Spain and England. First appearing in France, in the writings of Vauquelin, 1535–1607; reaching a superb development in Spain, in the great masterpiece of Cervantes, 1587–1616, it comes to its most general and signal expression in England in the seventeenth and eighteenth centuries.

In one form or another, satire may be said to have had a place in all nations and all ages, assuming special prominence at definite literary eras and among particular peoples. In fine, its historical origin is the best evidence of what we may call its philosophical or ethical origin; as this is seen, on the one hand, in human faults and follies open to correction, and, on the other, in the natural desire to act the part of personal censors of others. As long as the world is what it is in its sins and errors, and man is what he is in his taste for rebuke and ridicule, so long will there be a basis for satire and so long will its history be involved in human history. More than this, it is a species of style and literature as desirable as it is natural; in many instances the exclusive medium of truth; an element of authorship without some measure of which no writer can be said to be completely endowed for his work. Though, in its most telling forms, it is seen to be the natural gift of the author as a man, it yet lies, to some extent, within the sphere of the attainable, and is evoked by the experiences and teachings of surrounding life. All this conceded, however, it is to be added, that satire is a good servant, but an unsafe and often a tyrannical master. No writer can afford to be under its control. In common with wit as a type of literary expression, it must ever be kept within discreet and well-defined limits; under the sway of judgment, sympathy and purity of purpose. Thus guarded and guided, it may be used and ought to be used by every lover of the truth.

I. If we now inquire as to the distinctive Forms of Satire, we may regard them, in the most general sense, as twofold,—That of Ridicule and Humor; and that of Invective and Rebuke.

1. Of these, the first is expressed in what we technically term, the Serio-Comic, or Mock-Heroic. It is undoubtedly the typical form; the higher and the more subdued and less objectionable form. It deals in courteous innuendo; in quaint and epigrammatic allusion; in the ludicrous and laughable; modified, throughout, by the temper of kindliness. It possesses a good degree of what Thackeray calls "humanity," never hurling its missiles with intent to kill or even to wound. It is a species of pleasantry in disguise, far less severe than it seems to be, and often, as in the case of Falstaff and Pickwick, including itself among the objects of its address.

A brief recital of some of the world's leading satirists will fully illustrate this order, and reveal its prominence in literature. Horace, among the Latins, and Cervantes, of Spain, are notable exponents. In France, the name of Molière is especially prominent. In England and America, we may note a goodly number in the persons of Chaucer, Jonson, Butler, Burns, Addison, Hood, Jerrold, Sidney Smith, Lamb, De Quincey, Dickens, Thackeray, Holmes and Lowell. In the satirical pages of these and kindred authors, there is nothing of what Puttenham calls "dry mock," nothing bitter and cruel for the sake of inflicting pain and watching the distress of the sufferer. There is, on the contrary, a straightforward, open-hearted, well-tempered censorship of foibles and evils; an attack of the sin rather than the sinner and an ardent devotion to the best interests of the truth.

2. The Satire of Invective is of quite a different order and object; generally embodied in what is known as irony or sarcasm, a defiant onset upon flagrant forms of error. With reference to this species, it is essential to state, that it may be expressed in phases widely different from one another. There is at times a *righteous indignation* against the wrong. Rebuke is then administered where it is deserved and, yet, discreetly and in deference to personal feeling. Such is the invective of Scripture, as seen in the old prophets; in such an apostle as Paul, and in Christ himself, as he contemplates the character of the Pharisees of his day. It is seen in the language of all religious reformers, such as Knox, Luther and Savonarola; in such dauntless preachers as Latimer and the great court-chaplains of the reign of Louis XIV. In literary history, most distinctively, its characteristic features appear, as in Juvenal; in a succession of satirists on to the days of Beranger of France; in the pages of "Piers Plowman" of England, on through the writings of Pope and Collins and Thomas Carlyle. Far different from such satire as this is that which is *malicious* and vindictive in its tone, dealt out in deadly forms for the pleasure of the act rather than for the weal of men. This is invective on its baser side, and, though often productive of good, is so indirectly, and in spite of its method. It is full of spleen and venom, and bent

at all hazards on selfish ends. It is enough to mention such names as Boileau, Molière, Swift, Byron and Edgar Allan Poe, in his abuse of Longfellow, to show what is meant by literary malice and the opposing attitude which every high-minded author should assume respecting it. Those forms of satire are to be advocated which deal in ridicule and rebuke in a noble and catholic spirit, and which are never cynical and caustic at the expense of good taste and good feeling.

Viewing the forms of satire more specifically, as based on the particular *object* at the time, rather than on the *animus* of the author; we note three or four characteristic types—the Theological, or Religious, the Political, the Literary and the Social.

Theological. This first form is especially illustrated in later Continental and English authorship as distinct from the earlier and classical. The satires of Rabelais and Erasmus, in the latter part of the fifteenth century, may be said to have been of this order, as they vented their indignation against the penances, pilgrimages and corrupt priesthood of the times. In the pages of Langlande, author of "Piers Plowman," there is seen the earliest extended example of English satire in the form of religious rebuke. Partly political, as directed against the corruptions of the nobility; and, partly, social, as condemning the prevalent morality of the age; it was, mainly, theological and ethical, as bearing upon the open vices of the clergy and the gross abuses of the Papal church. In his preference of conscience and reason to Romish dogma, his emphatic exaltation of the Scriptures above all human councils, and of purity of life above external ceremony, he was doing the same necessary work that Wiclif was aiming to do in other forms, and thus preparing the way for the Protestant Reformation in England in the days of Queen Elizabeth. Samuel Butler's "Hudibras" was an indirect attack upon the Puritans in the form of the mock-heroic; similar, in some of its features, to the attack made by Cervantes upon the knight-errantry of Spain. In the pages of John Dryden, we come to one of the most pronounced of English satirists. In his "Hind and Panther," we have his best work along the lines of theological criticism; the "milk-white Hind," representing the Church of Rome, and the "Panther," "the lady of the spotted muff," representing the Church of England. Other religious orders, as Presbyterians, Independents, Friends, Anabaptists, Arians and Free Thinkers, are symbolized, respectively, by the wolf, bear, hare, boar, fox and ape. James the Second is the Lion; the Lollards are "Wiclif's brood." Christ is "the blessed Pan," and so on through this "Reineke Fuchs" of English verse. The poem is simply a defence of the Papacy, on behalf of King James in his ambitious schemes as to an English hirerarchy, and is marked throughout by that incisiveness and pertinence of statement for which its author was justly famed. Of a somewhat similar character and motive was

Jonathan Swift's "Tale of a Tub," in which, under the guise of Peter, Martin and Jack, he deals out his sarcasm relative, respectively, to Romanism, Anglicanism, and the doctrines of the Dissenters. A little later on, we note, in Doctor Johnson's "London" and his "Vanity of Human Wishes," conspicuous examples of ethical satire on the despondent side, as representing those disappointments and, often, fruitless struggles of human life with which the author himself was so familiar.

2. Political. In this particular sphere, satire frequently appears in its most pronounced forms. Frequently mingled, as in Langlande and others, with theological references, it has a province of its own and includes unique examples. In "The Peace" of Aristophanes, it is seen, as he treats of the Peloponnesian War; in France, in the person of Beranger, it finds a signal expression in his invectives against the tyranny of Napoleonic rule. Cicero against Catiline illustrates it. Arbuthnot, of England, exemplifies it, as in his, "Law Is a Bottomless Pit," he refers to the civil discords connected with the French War, on to the Treaty of Utrecht. Gray, in his "Beggars' Opera," is bold enough to satirize the English court, of the early Georgian era. Andrew Marvell, of Cromwellian days, in his "Hodge's Vision," fought for liberty of conscience in church and state. Perhaps the most pungent and effective production of this order is found in the "Drapier's Letters" of Dean Swift, published in 1724, directed against Wood's half-

pence, so called, as an outrageous monopoly of profit against the common interests of Ireland. Macaulay, in his essays on "Machiavelli," "The Civil Disabilities of the Jews," "Warren Hastings" and "Frederick the Great," indulges in those home thrusts, of which he was so expert a master; as, also, De Quincey, in such papers as, "Whiggism," "The Cæsars," and "Charlemagne," fails not to embrace the opportunity offered him in the line of political satire.

3. Literary. When we turn to satire of this order, ancient and modern times are full of illustrations of it. The satires of Ennius himself were of this specific cast in the line of scenic representation. Aristophanes, in the "Clouds," ridicules the sophists, while Horace, Persius, Martial and Rabelais deal, more or less largely, in reflections on authors and authorship. The poems of Joseph Hall, who is cited in English Literary History as the first English satirist, in chronological order, directed his lines against the style of the times. Dryden, in his "Mac Flecknoe," gave to the English public of his day a serio-comic poem, full to the brim of literary sarcasm, excelled only by the "Dunciad" of Pope, his successor, in which masterly poem the third and fourth rate authors of the age were handled in a merciless manner, and, thereby, transmitted to history, with some degree of notoriety. Next to these in pungency and satirical merit, is Pope's "Rape of the Lock," which, after its kind, as a mock-heroic poem, has no approximate rival in

any modern tongue. In this particular *rôle* of literary satirists, the name of Swift again appears, in his "Battle of the Books," wherein the war is waged, as to the comparative merits of the ancient and the modern learning. Churchill, in his "Rosciad," fulminates against the stage with the incisiveness of Collins himself. Boileau of France, in his unsparing thrusts against Madame de Scudèry and others, attacked what he regarded as the bad taste of the time and the inane piety of England, Spain and Italy. Voltaire, with a spirit even more bitter, vented his godless raillery against Shakespeare and less distinguished authors and, in his dramas, gave full scope to what have been well called "his declamatory tirades." Edward Young, in his "Epistles to Pope," indulges in sarcastic slurs against contemporaneous authorship. Arbuthnot, in his "Martinus Scriblerus," ridicules the abuse of learning. Macaulay and De Quincey, Lamb and Sidney Smith, Byron, Hood, Arnold and Lowell write satirically of books and authors, style and language. In such a periodical as, the "Edinburgh Review," and, especially, in such invectives as are found in "English Bards and Scotch Reviewers," we have as signal an instance as could be afforded us, of literary satire. In fact, literary criticism is, in many of its phases, but a form of ironical address, either in the line of humorous banter or in that of stern rebuke and dissent. Those quarrels of authors, to which Mr. Disraeli has called our attention, are largely due to this free indulgence in literary censorship. Even when not acrid and caustic, they take the form of comment and rejoinder. The pen is an instrument that cuts two ways and, in the hands of a master, may be made the agent of literary compliment or criticism.

4. Social. This fourth and final form of satire may be said to be the most characteristic and most abundant, found in all literatures and often combining, in one generic expression, all other forms possible to language. This was pre-eminently the Roman or classical form, as seen in the pages of Lucilius who, as a satirist of men and manners, of social and common life, is justly regarded as the first Latin satirist, if not, indeed, the first of literary history. It was, however, in Juvenal and his school that this unique species reached its culmination, not surpassed since in the virulence of its spirit, as it has never been more signally demanded by the social character of the age. Had this old Roman censor dealt out his teachings in the modified and courteous manner of the Horatian poems, his mission would have been but half fulfilled and flagrant evils would have passed unnoticed and unrebuked. Rabelais and Erasmus, Vaugelin and Regnier followed along this line. Cervantes, in his "Don Quixote," reached the acme of this social criticism on the ludicrous side and effected, by good-natured innuendo, what others might have reached by calumny and mockery. Dryden and Butler, Pope and Marvell, combined this special form with

the political and literary forms, while it is reserved for the English essayists and novelists, from the days of De Foe on to Thomas Carlyle, to give us the best examples of social satire. Swift, in his "Gulliver's Travels"; Addison and Steele, in the "Spectator" and "Tatler"; Johnson, in the "Rambler" and "Rasselas"; Lamb, in his "Essays of Elia"; Macaulay, in his numerous miscellanies; Hood, in his "Whims and Oddities"; Douglas Jerrold, in his essays; and De Quincey, in such papers as "French and English Manners," "The Juggernaut of Social Life" and, "Murder Considered as One of the Fine Arts," all exhibit, more or less fully, this satirical treatment of men and manners. Prominent over all essayists, in this regard, is the dark-visaged, reflective and cynical Carlyle, the self-appointed censor of his age; living and dying in sadness of spirit, in that he was a herald of truth to a generation deaf to his message.

It is, however, within the sphere of English Fiction, that English authors have done their best work in the line of social satire. In De Foe, Goldsmith, Richardson, Fielding, Bulwer, Reade, Trollope, Dickens, Charlotte Brontë, George Eliot, Hawthorne and Howells, and, above all, in Mr. Thackeray, satire of the social order has come to its maximum of excellence, and we scarcely hope for better illustrations of its forms. Not theology, nor politics, nor letters, but human life itself, in its every-day dress and bearing; man himself, as he figures at home, in the street, in the shop and in society, is the most unique province of satire, as it is, also, its most prolific occasion and incentive.

We call attention to the *need* of satire in all ages, and its special need at present. Its ethical origin, as we have seen, in the follies and frailties natural to the race, will ensure its necessity so long as human nature is what it is. In the guise of malicious and bitter mockery, as in Poe and Swinburne, it has no place in any age or nation, however provocative of it the existing evils may be. In the guise, however, of the ludicrous and the laughable, as seen in the pages of Lamb and Holmes and the popular humorists of the day, it has an appropriate sphere among us and may be made an adjutant of the truth itself. Such are the whims, the high conceits, the puerile extremes and senseless exhibitions of modern life, that the opportunity for ridicule is far too patent to be lost, so that he who is able to utilize his gifts in that direction has, thereby, a call to such a ministry. All forms of presumption, theological, religious, political, literary, social and individual, need positive rebuke, and, if removable in no other manner, must be actually laughed off the stage, or scorned off amid the plaudit of the populace. No man can read the doctrinal, civil and literary discussions of the day, or keep his eye open to the ridiculous *rôle* so constantly played in what is called, society, and not make an effort, at least, to ventilate his personal protest and contempt in some accepted species of satirical address.

If we turn to that kind of satire which is an indignant and a well-deserved rebuke of outrageous wrongs in church and state and letters and life, what limit can be fixed, in such an age as this, to the number or the boldness of the invectives that should be discharged. In this respect, Wendell Phillips, Charles Sumner, and the Earl of Beaconsfield have done invaluable service in the province of statecraft. Mr. Carlyle, despite his bad temper, has done a similar service in the sphere of literature and common life, particularly against all shams and abuses, manfully contending for the reign of righteousness and order and personal candor. Are we not needing in modern American life worthy successors of these prophets of truth? Are we not needing, in politics, some modern Beranger or Swift, and, in society, a Juvenal himself, to castigate prevailing errors and vices and frauds and bring in, once again, the era of reform? Is there not ample room, indeed, for another "Dunciad," in the pages of which the presumptuous versifiers and writers of the day, shall be pilloried for all time? Even in theology itself, the senseless controversies between the Hind and the Panther, the Bear and the Wolf, the Fox and the Ape continue, and entice the pen of the ready writer to record his deserved dissent. So long as, in the regions of doctrinal dispute, men are pleased to exalt creeds and forms and external rites of the church to the plane of vital piety; so long as literature finds a ready reading in proportion to its lack of sterling mental fibre; so long as patriotism has so largely succumbed to partisanship, and the very name of justice is travestied in municipal and national councils; so long, moreover, as society is seeking to outdo all its former follies and to put hollow courtesy in the place of character, it is, certainly, more than fitting that some Savonarola or Molière should arise whose satirical skill may be equal to his moral courage, and in the name of God and truth, brand evil things with evil names and seek to rectify the wrong.

Nothing can be said against the need and wholesomeness of satire as an element of style, wielded by a hand able to wield it, and, in its most pronounced expressions, tempered with a due amount of Christian charity. In a country as democratic and spacious as our own; with its rapidly increasing population and diversities of interest, there is special danger lest the use of satire be taken, in the main, out of the control of those best fitted to wield it, and be given over, as a matter of expediency, to a less competent constituency. This, in fact, is the very process now at work among us, and the modern American Press is fast becoming the only accredited censor of wrongs and abuses, follies and blunders. Such a monopoly of satire by the public press is attended with manifest dangers in the line of a one-sided, superficial, and, often, malicious criticism of men and customs. Such a procedure goes far to despoil satire of that dignified bearing that it has borne in all nations, when mainly confined to the province of literature, and thus vitally partaking of that good name which such a literature is presumed to bear.

We, therefore, urge a prompt resistance of this dangerous tendency, on the part of all who have literary influence, and a decided endeavor to reinstate satirical style in its earlier prominence as a distinctively scholarly art. In one or another of its legitimate forms, every student of style and letters should seek to cultivate and express it, in the course of his literary life. Based to some degree on an innate sense of the ludicrous and an innate abhorrence of the evil, its cultivation as an art is feasible, founded, as it is, on the further cultivation of the faculty of observation; on an ever-widening knowledge of the world; on a discerning study of policies and systems and a conscientious desire to conserve the interests of truth. Some follies cannot be corrected and some wrongs cannot be righted by the ordinary methods of address and appeal. They must be reached and remedied by unique procedure. Satire is as old as the world in which it lives and the sins and follies it rebukes. As civilization advances in right directions and Christianity has sway over men, its area ought to be perceptibly narrowed and its forms and function limited.

For its final and complete abolition, however, we cannot rationally look till truth and righteousness come to their universal supremacy in the far-off days of millennial glory; till Beauty triumph over the Beast, and Satan succumb to Christ.

THE SATIRICAL STYLE.

Examples.

One great advantage proposed by the abolishing of Christianity is, that it would very much enlarge and establish liberty of conscience. . . . which is still too much limited by priestcraft. For it is confidently reported that the young gentlemen of real hopes, bright wit and profound judgment who, upon a thorough examination of causes and effects, and by the mere force of natural abilitics. . . . having made a discovery that there was no God, generously communicated their thoughts for the good of the public, were, some time ago, and I know not upon what obsolete law, broke for blasphemy. As it has been wisely observed, if persecution once begins, no man alive knows how far it may reach or where it will end.—*Swift's "Argument Against Abolishing Christianity."*

I will venture to give to the reader two little pieces of advice. The first is, by no means to credit the widespread report that these seventeenth century Puritans were superstitious, crack-brained persons. . . . Cant was not fashionable at all; that stupendous invention of "Speech for the purpose of concealing thought," was not yet made. A man wagging the tongue of him, as if it were the clapper of a bell to be rung for economic purposes. . . . would at that date have awakened all the horror in men's minds. The use of the human tongue then was other than it now is.—*Carlyle's "Cromwell."*

Here is now an argument to prove the matter against the preachers. Here was preaching against covetousness all the last year and, the next summer, followed rebellion. Ergo, preaching against covetousness was the cause of the rebellion—a goodly argument. Well then, quoth Master More, what think you to be the cause of these shelves and flats that stop up Sandwich haven? Forsooth, sir, quoth he, I am an old man. I think that Tenterton steeple is the cause of Goodwin Sands. Before that Tenterton steeple was in building, there was no manner of speaking of any flats or sands that stopped the haven; therefore I think that Tenterton steeple is the cause of the decay of Sandwich haven. So, to my purpose, is preaching of God's word the cause of rebellion.—*Hugh Latimer's "Sermons."*

As I grew up and observed the actions of men, I thought I met with many who gave too much for the whistle. When I saw any one too ambitious of court favor, I have said to myself—This man gives too much for his whistle. If I see one fond of fine clothes, fine furniture, fine equipages, all above his fortune, for which he contracts debts and ends his career in prison—alas, says I, he has paid dear, very dear, for his whistle.—*Benjamin Franklin's "Works."*

CHAPTER VIII.

STYLE AND HUMOR.

(The Humorous Style.)

THE necessity of the humorous element in what Mr. Whipple calls, literature and life, is at once apparent. We pass, by natural and unavoidable transitions, from "grave to gay; from lively to severe." The "Il Penseroso" of Milton demanded his "L'Allegro." As Mr. Emerson expresses it, in his readable paper on, "The Comic," "A taste for fun is almost universal in our species, which is the only joker in nature. A perception of the comic appears to be an essential element in a fine character. Wherever the intellect is constructive, it will be found. We feel the absence of it as a defect in the noblest and most oracular soul. It is a tie of sympathy with other men, a pledge of sanity, and a protection from those perverse tendencies and gloomy insanities in which fine intellects sometimes lose themselves. A rogue alive to the ludicrous is still convertible."

This is suggestive language from such a philosophical writer as Emerson, and reveals the fact, which it is important to emphasize, that the grounds of humor, in man and in authorship, lie back of the man and the book, in the original construction of things; arising, as dramatic representation arises, by a primal and an irresistible necessity. There is a philosophy of humor as well as of sobriety, and of the one because of the other. As has been truthfully said—"The ludicrous side of life, like the serious side, has its literature, and it is a literature of untold wealth." There is a "time to laugh and to dance," just as assuredly as there is a "time to weep and to mourn." The one is, moreover, just as essential to the expression and maintenance of character as the other.

In this respect, at least, the English Puritans of the days of the Commonwealth were wrong, as developing but one side of the double nature of man, and Lord Macaulay must be partly sanctioned in his stringent criticism of their method and spirit. Eliminate humor from any society or literature, and a factor so supremely vital has been removed that no other possible substitute can fill its place. It is as old as human nature and as new, and, if not allowed scope and function along the lines of its natural manifestation, will avenge its suppression in multiplied abnormal forms.

I. If we inquire as to the final and paramount *object* that humor has in view, as one of the elements of all good style, we must call it, *entertainment* or *pleasure*. It is precisely what Mr. Whipple states it to be, when he speaks of the "Literature of Mirth." It is what the old Saxons called, the gleeful and gladsome side of life and art. Its central personage is given us in Milton's

> "Jest and youthful jollity; heart-easing Mirth,
> Sport that wrinkled Care derides,
> And Laughter holding both his sides."

In a word, its object is to act as "a balance wheel in our metaphysical structure;" as a corrective of extreme tendencies in the direction of the introspective and sedate; to be, in a writer's style, an ever-present witness for the cheerful and hopeful, and so, by protest and appeal, to keep the didactic and dispassionate within proper limits.

Nor are we to be misled by the use of terms, when we pronounce pleasure to be the end of humor. There are endless grades and forms of pleasure, some of which are eliminated by the very presence of the genuinely humorous, while some are seen to coexist with it. The pleasure which it seeks and secures is rational and refined, an order and a measure of gladness befitting intelligent and cultured men, who love truth and purity more than questionable entertainment. It is not too much to say, that in humor thus viewed there are intellectual and ethical elements, sharply distinguishing it in its object and character from that which often passes for it. We have already quoted from

Emerson in confirmation of such a view. Mr. Whipple tells us "that it was the glory of Addison and Steele to redeem polite literature from moral depravity by showing that wit could chime merrily in with the voice of virtue." Thackeray holds to this same high ideal, and enforces the realization of it. In his "English Humorists," when speaking of Jonathan Swift, he says, that humor means something more than "laughter;" that it appeals to other senses than that of "ridicule;" that it is the business of the humorist to "moralize;" to be the "week-day preacher," to his readers. Thackeray himself rarely lost sight of this fundamental object of humor, so that, in his most romping, rollicking dealing with the English life of his day, he maintained his self-respect, his status as an author, and never condescended to the tricks of the mountebank to arouse an ignorant and a low-minded constituency. It is to this that the "Spectator" refers, in one of its anonymous papers, in sentiments worthy of Addison, "that ridicule is never stronger than when it is concealed in gravity."

Nor is it meant, here, that the art of pleasantry should defeat its own ends by a decorum and expression correct to a fault. No reference is here made to what Mr. Stedman, in criticism of Poe, calls "grave-yard humor, which sends a chill down our backs," but to a natural, normal, rational and manly purpose in the use of such an agent, all the more necessary because it is capable of such flagrant abuse.

II. As to the *relations* of humor to other forms of literature and style, it may be said, in general, that it touches all possible forms. Just because it arises out of the inherent constitution of man and society, there is nothing human that is alien to it, and there is no authorship that is wholly free from its direct or indirect influence. It is thus in place to call attention, here, to those few phases or departments of literary art with which it has especially to do, though, as having an area of its own, it must be kept distinct from them.

1. Humor and Wit. These are terms that, by the use of language and common consent, have come to be employed somewhat interchangeably, the implication being that where one is found, the other is. This by no means follows, while the scholar, and, especially, the writer, must never fail to accord to humor the superior place and function.

Mr. Whipple, in his suggestive way, has so admirably set forth the differences of these two qualities, to the advantage of humor, that a few of these contrasts may be noted. "Wit exists by sympathy; humor, by antipathy. Wit lashes external appearances or cunningly exaggerates single foibles into character; humor glides into the heart of its object, looks lovingly on the infirmities it detects, and represents the whole man. Wit is abrupt, darting, scornful, and tosses its analogies in your face; humor is slow and sly, insinuating its fun into your heart. Wit is negative, analytical, destructive; humor is creative. Wit, when earnest, has the earnestness of passion, seeking to destroy; humor has the earnestness of affection, and would lift up what is seemingly low, into charity and love." No careful reader of modern literature, and, especially, of English, can fail to notice such salient differences as these to which the American critic calls attention. There is such a quality of written language as mere wit, and such a character as a mere wit; dealing chiefly, if not exclusively, in external, verbal quibblings; playing the *rôle* of the punster; craftily taking advantage of every possible perversion in word or phrase; producing a style, if it can be called a style, which has little to commend it to the high regard of scholars. This is what the "Spectator" calls "burlesque humor," or "epigrammatic wit," the implication being, that it is humor of the lowest order, in that the epigram must, at all hazards, be pointed.

There have been English writers, such as Douglas Jerrold and Sidney Smith, in whose pages wit has risen to its best forms, and is seen in close alliance with humor. Such examples are, however, rare; these two qualities being oftener found to exist separately, if not, indeed, in an inverse ratio, as with Voltaire and Rabelais, Swift and Poe. In a word, the vital difference between them is, that the one has an *intellectual* element of which the other is devoid. "The command of humor," says Mr. Stedman, has distinguished men whose genius was both high and broad." "It is one of the marks," as Emerson tells us, "of a constructive intellect." It is one of the multiform expressions of personal genius in letters, as much so as is an epic poem or a masterly effort in prose. As one of our critics quaintly expresses it, when speaking of the etymological meaning of humor as; moisture, "It is the very juice of the mind, oozing from the brain." It has a distinctively mental cast, differentiating it from wit as unintellectual. If wit is a play on words, humor is a play on ideas, making, in its expression and appreciation, the nobler order of mind.

2. Humor and Satire. Here, again, we employ terms that, in a sense, imply each other. They have some common characteristics and, as a matter of literary history, are often seen to coexist in somewhat similar measures of expression. Cervantes, in his matchless romance, is a satirist and a humorist in one. It would be difficult to state in which of these departments of literary expression he excels or where the line of division is to be drawn. Other examples, in European and English letters, might be cited. In the chapter on Satire, attention is called to the two leading forms of satire—that of ridicule and that of rebuke. It is with the former of these that humor is closely connected, so that excellence in the one implies excellence in the other. Horace, Molière, Chaucer, Ben Jonson, Samuel Butler, Addison, Hood, Lowell and Holmes clearly evince this union of gifts and styles.

When we speak of the satire of invective and indignant protest, as seen in Juvenal, Lucian, Savonarola, Voltaire, Swift, Carlyle and Poe, we can readily discern that we are dealing with a form of satire that has no normal relation to humor, but may be said to be incompatible with its proper exercise. We thus reach the distinctive difference between the two qualities as they affect style when we say, that the one is considerate, the other, regardless of interest; the one uses beneficent means toward beneficent ends, while the other has no scruples as to means or ends, if so be it satisfies its own selfish aims.

There is, perhaps, no sphere in which the natural relation of humor to satire is better seen than in that of pure fiction and the comic drama. In these departments, each is at its best, and they interact to common aims. Hence, no better examples of what might be called, humorous satire and satiric humor, can be found than in such authors as Dickens, Thackeray, Shakespeare and Massinger. Such portraitures as are given us in, "Dombey and Son," and the "Pickwick Papers;" in "Vanity Fair," and "The Newcomes"; in "The Merry Wives of Windsor," and the "Comedy of Errors," and "A New Way to Pay Old Debts," are all full of pleasantry and personal allusion in happy combination. No one can rightly find fault with what Mr. Pickwick says, or with Falstaff, unless, indeed, he is determined to be at war with the world. So pacific and conciliatory is the tone and so adroitly is the language tempered to the existing conditions of human nature that we cannot take offence where no offence is intended. All that is necessary is, to enter heartily into the hilarity of the hour and apply the lessons that are so ingenuously given. In some of the subordinate divisions of the drama, such as the Farce, this union is seen in special form, while comedy and fiction, throughout, might not incorrectly be classified under the satirical and humorous. Having a common origin in the nature of man, they develop, in this respect, along common lines, and may be examined by the student of style as a twofold manifestation of one and the same generic principle.

III. As to the *forms* which Humor may assume, suffice it to say, that they are as varied as the nature, needs and conditions of man. As has been said, it is "Protean." Mr. Whipple, in one of his papers, gives us some of the varied phases which it may assume, as seen in different natures and authors—in Göethe, Pope, Moore, Steele, Goldsmith, Hawthorne and others. The forms differ as widely as human personality differs.

If we examine a little more closely, we will discover two or three forms in which the best humor seems, as a law, to manifest itself in style.

1. The Humor of Ridicule. This satisfies what Emerson calls "the taste for fun." This is the particular province of jest and mirth and apt

rejoinder. It is the domain ot the laughable, whence Milton's

> "Loathed Melancholy,
> Of Cerberus and blackest midnight born,"

is forever banished.

Cervantes, in his superb caricature of the knight-errantry of the Middle Ages, has no superior in this direction, whose exquisite pleasantry is partially repeated in the pages of Butler's "Hudibras." This ridicule is at times exhibited in the line of the odd, quaint and grotesque, as in some of the writings of the eccentric Burton and Fuller. What the old writers called the "incongruity" of the humorous, as a necessary feature of it, is here apparent—incongruity of profession and practice; of word and idea; of antecedents and present conditions; of personal appearance and mental endowments; of time and place and general environment. Humor takes advantage of anything outside the province of the regular and natural and expected, making much of its capital out of ill-adjusted conditions.

2. The Humor of Reflection. This is a form equally potent and still more attractive. The tone is subdued, sensitive and often emotive. It is "fun and feeling" combined, a kind of compromise, on the part of the humorist, between the tendency to deal sharply with his subject and his more kindly instincts. Some of the finest exhibitions of the humorous style are in this province, as in Sir

Walter Scott, Goldsmith's "Vicar of Wakefield"; Lamb's "Essays of Elia" and Irving's "Miscellanies."

So pronounced, at times, is this type that it takes the form of the pensive or contemplative, a deep, impassioned cast of sentiment and language. If the humorist, at such times, must be comic, he retains his meditative manner by being serio-comic, not infrequently erring by mingling too much sadness with his mirth. Such authors as Hood and Sterne, and even De Quincey, have erred in this regard, the error itself only confirming the view, that ridicule is not the only form of humor, but that the ethical and emotive often assert themselves in a sensitive and sympathetic manner, thus preserving humor in style from degenerating into the baser forms, or even confining itself to the purely laughable.

IV. The way is now open for a more particular examination of the Elements of Humor.

It is important to state, at the outset, that any such thing as an exhaustive analysis of this quality of style is as impossible as it is inexpedient. This is so just because it is humor, defying definition and elucidation beyond a very narrow limit. As beauty, taste, sublimity and similar notions: its real nature can best be determined either through an appreciative study of it, as seen in open form, or by a personal experience of what it is. Mr. Lowell, in his paper on the great Spanish humorist, remarks—"I shall not trouble you with any labored analysis of humor. If you wish to know what humor is, I should say, read 'Don Quixote.' It is something in mind and art not discernible by the senses, nor is it reducible to syllogistic statement or philosophic formula. It is what it is, and refuses to reveal its innermost self fully to the inquisitive critic. Literary criticism, on its technical side, has but little to do with it. It shines by its own light; pleases in its own way; knows its own mission; avenges its own slights. All that we can do or wish to do, as students of style, is to indicate a few leading features which shine conspicuously in it, and which, being seen, afford a safe criterion by which to judge of that which remains unrevealed.

1. The first of these elements is, Surprise. In humor, as nowhere else, it is the unexpected that occurs. In so far as this is concerned, it is allied to wit, though high above it. The surprise is always in the line of the credible and natural, and however much it may startle us, never shocks and staggers and stuns us. It never gives us what Whipple quaintly calls, "a sudden jerk of the understanding," but in its most novel manifestations, preserves the proprieties and satisfies the sense of dignity and decorum. This element of surprise in humor may be best indicated by calling it a kind of half-revelation and half-concealment of the thought; these together producing the desired effect, which could not be produced by full disclosure. It is only glimpses that are given us,

purposely leaving it to us to fill out the scene or statement. Herein lie its attractiveness and effect. Mr. Emerson, in his "Essay on the Comic," lays special stress on this, as he says, "The essence of all comedy seems to be an honest or a well-intended *halfness;* a non-performance of what is intended to be performed, at the same time that one is giving loud pledges of performance. The frustrated expectation, the break of continuity in the intellect is comedy;" is, he would say, humor. As in sublimity, obscurity or partial manifestation for added effect is a prime element, so, here, there is a legitimate "halfness" for the sake of final wholeness. In this respect, humor carries out the Tennysonian principle—

> "For words, like Nature, half reveal
> And half conceal the Soul within."

To this extent, at least, Talleyrand's half-truth, "that language is the art of concealing thought"—has a place and an application. It conceals as well as reveals.

2. Spontaneity. If there is any one type or quality of style where the feature of naturalness must be preserved as all important, it is in humor. It is nothing if not natural. In the language of another, it is the "overflow of strength," the overflow, we may add, of heart, mind and soul; the unrestrained and unrestrainable expression of the inner man. It is just as free and self-directing as the involuntary bodily functions, and is something

other than itself just to the degree in which it is restricted. Wherever else literary students may disagree, they agree, without exception, here, that spontaneousness is the soul of humor. As Mr. Stedman states it—"Humor is congenital," and he rightly criticises Poe for working on the "delusion that humor comes by works and not by inborn gift." It is because of this that we find it impossible fully to dissect and explain it. No effort of the intellect or will can evoke it when it is not ready to appear, in its own way, by "spontaneous generation." No teachings of the schools; no canons of criticism will induce it from without in a nature in which it is not primarily at home. That author must have rare powers of concealment who can, in any sense, use it at second hand as if it were his by original endowment. There is such a thing as "mother-wit" or mother-humor, and there is no other worth the name—an innate, intuitive habit of mind and order of style, which bears upon every lineament of it the evidence of its origin and excellence.

3. Delicacy. Reference is here made to that particular form of the humorous style which is termed, the subdued or contemplative; as seen, for example, in the fiction of Hawthorne and the writings of the old Knickerbocker School. Though partially present in the humor of ridicule, this delicacy of cast and touch is especially seen in this less demonstrative type. It is pure, chaste and affable in its character; sensitive, almost to a fault,

to any possible violation of ethical or literary law. Mr. Stedman, in speaking of Holmes, possibly refers to this feature, when he says—"As a humorist, he was among the first to teach his countrymen that pathos is an equal part of true humor . . . . that jest is redeemed from coarseness by emotion." It is this conspicuous absence of "coarseness" to which we allude in speaking of the delicacy of humor. It is what Mr. Arnold would call, "urbanity." Mr. Disraeli would thus place it among the "amenities" of literature, whereby the way is graded and smoothed for the reception of the truth beneath the humor. If there is much in genuine pleasantry that is sweet and satisfying to a cultured taste, it is largely owing to this winsome element, whereby all the rough edges of thought and language are removed, and the truth is made palatable. Reference has been made to Hawthorne. What appreciative reader of that gifted author has failed to note the delicacy of his humor; so subdued, graceful and happily expressed; so meditative, and yet so cheerful; so searching and subtle, and yet so gentle; so ethical, yet so attractive, so felicitous in tone and in the general type of its art, that modern literature has yet to surpass it. Serious, reverent and quiet in all his utterances; so that no one would dare impugn his character, or trespass, in the least, upon the sanctity of his innermost life and habit, he is yet as sportive as a child at play, and reassures us, at every step, of his personal welcome. This is nature, and it is, also, the perfection of art, a second nature, expressive of the first. Humor, in any of its forms, is recompensing but when expressed with this delicacy of subject-matter and of manner becomes, indeed, the most pleasing and attractive product of literary work.

4. Individuality. The very idea of humor involves that of personality. A writer may more lawfully be imitated in any other department of written expression. When he comes to the art of pleasantry for the sake of pleasantry, it must be the man himself and no other one, who speaks to us. One of the most palpable distinctions between wit and humor is at this point; in that the one is dependent and adaptive of borrowed suggestion, while the other is purely original.

This characteristic is evident whether we have reference to individual or national humor. All the great humorists, such as Cervantes, Molière, Lamb, Dickens and Irving, have been such in their own way. No one would confound the pleasantry of Doctor Johnson with that of De Quincey; or that of Addison with that of Carlyle, or that of Hawthorne with that of Holmes. So in humor as nationally exhibited. How marked the difference between the somewhat slow and measured mirth of the North Europeans as a class and the quick, epigrammatic pleasantry of Southern Europe. Mr. Bryce, in his "American Commonwealth," writing of American traits says: "All the world knows that they are a humorous people, as conspicuously the purveyors of humor to the nineteenth century as the French were the purveyors of wit to the eighteenth." The most casual observer detects certain cardinal features of British humor as distinct from American, nor is he slow to see that the broad, serious manner of the Englishman or the Scotchman is something quite different from the dash and flash of Celtic humor as expressed in Ireland and Wales. Thackeray, in his "Irish Sketches," has given us choice specimens of these characteristics, while such Celtic anthors as Goldsmith and Moore personally illustrate them. In so far as Carlyle was a humorist as distinct from a satirist, he was wholly himself, and in this respect satisfied one of the prime conditions of success in the art of pleasing.

5. We note, as the final and crowning element of Humor, its Geniality. It is full of "good feeling and fellow feeling;" open-hearted and whole-souled; sympathetic and generous; unwilling to inflict a wound, even when indulging in its most extreme exercise, and never so satisfied as when it adds pleasure to pleasure in the experience of the object of its mirth. There is no place where the humorist appears to better advantage than here, or where humor, as a phase of style, better fulfills its primary purpose. Such a writer aims to be on good terms with all mankind; to note their follies and foibles with a charitable eye; to impart cheer and courage where they did not, heretofore, exist; often, as Falstaff of old, making itself the object of its mirth. Certain names always suggest

themselves as we contemplate the genial side of the humorous style—Walton, Lamb, Addison, Christopher North, Burns, Dickens and Irving: men "full of the milk of human kindness," in whom the heart always asserted its claims and who positively refused to be in high glee at the expense of any one's character or feelings. Herein lies much of the charm of Chaucer, who, at the very opening of our national letters, happily set the form for all later writers and made it a possible and desirable thing for English style, ever afterward, to be humorous and yet hearty.

Genuine pleasantry, thus conceived, cannot live in the presence of the captious and cynical; the morose and morbid, but finds its home in the tenderest affections of the soul, and seeks to do good to men by adding to their rational happiness. It accepts the world at its best and aims to make it still better; fully believes that to every man enough of the disciplinary and depressing will come, and that he is a real friend of the race who gives scope to his most generous impulses and, when he can get rid of care and wrong in no other way, laughs them out of countenance by the sheer force of pleasantry.

We note, at this point, the striking absence of the humorous in the character and style of many of the ablest writers of English Prose: in Hooker, Bacon, Milton, Hume, Gibbon, Burke, Thomas Arnold, Landor, Coleridge, Southey, Wordsworth, Matthew Arnold, as in most of the leading historians, essayists and even novelists of the England of to-day. Fiction, itself the natural home of humor, in its present religious tendency, on the one hand, and its sensual tendency, on the other, is fast eliminating this happy, cheerful tone. Whether we read the ethical philosophy of George Eliot or the debasing sentiments of Emile Zola, we are out of the region of exhilarating mirth, and must, first, be sober and then sad.

Some would refer this state of things to the introspective habit of the student of literature; some, to peculiar historical antecedents and environment, while others, as Mr. Taine, would refer its absence in England to the saturnine temperament of the race and their unduly ethical nature and habit. There is some truth, perhaps, in each of these explanations, while the fact remains that, in English Literature and Style, the spirit of genuine humor is not sufficiently pronounced. Our leading humorists stand out by way of contrast, and but serve to reveal the intensely serious manner in which most of our writers prosecute their work. How strikingly is this seen in such writers as, Shairp, Minto, Patterson, Nichol, Ainger, Courthope and others, holding themselves, as a rule, strictly to the letter and the line of the authorship; rarely venturing out into fanciful excursion or daring to interrupt the severe sobriety of the narrative by playful allusion and pleasantry. There is danger, here, lest the reading public revolt and the "literature of mirth," so held in abeyance, give way, at length, by violent reaction, to the fast and loose indulgences of the days of the Stuarts. The genius of Shakespeare is nowhere more apparent than in the way in which he relieves the body of his dramatic verse by the humorous quality, so that, even in tragedy itself, we have not always to hold our breath under the terrible pressure of the unfolding plot. It is this quality, among others, that keeps his plays alive and will so keep them for all time.

Style is the expression of thought, but it is more. It is the expression of the man behind the thought; the revelation of human consciousness, experience and aspiration. In the nature of the case, therefore, it must run up and down the entire scale of human life, touching every chord and giving voice to every sentiment. If the scientific and philosophic have their claims, the entertaining has its claims; partly, on grounds of literary variety, but, mainly, because, as Emerson tells us, "its absence is a defect." Even so didactic a writer as Plutarch contended that philosophy and life alike needed the element of mirth.

The thousands of Americans who sat with enthusiastic interest at the feet of Charles Dickens to listen to the recitation of his own productions, did so, chiefly, on the ground that he had done so much by his humorous writings to brighten English fiction and human life. It was an ingenuous testimony to the beneficent ministry of pleasantry in authorship. It will be difficult, indeed, to say which we could the better spare from our vernacular letters, Bacon's "Novum Organum," or Lamb's "Essays of Elia," Addison's criticism of "Paradise Lost" or his portraiture of Sir Roger de Coverley; Irving's "Life of Washington," or his "Knickerbocker Sketches," Webster's "Orations" or the "Biglow Papers," the judicial gravity of Hamilton or the jollity of Holmes—in a word, fact or humor; history or comedy.

We are, happily, shut up to no such alternative, as we discern, in the wide diversity of thought and life, a proper place for each, and, also, discern that the principle of comprehensive unity insists that each shall be given its rightful function in the ever-widening province of literature and style.

THE HUMOROUS STYLE.

Examples.

There are two sorts of dangers which hang over railroads; the one, retail dangers, where individuals are concerned; the other, wholesale dangers, where the whole train is put in jeopardy. But the most absurd of all legislative enactments is this hemiplegian law—an act of Parliament to protect one side of the body and not the other.

The first person of rank who is killed will put everything in order. I hope it will not be one of the bench of bishops; but should it be so destined, let the burnt bishop—the unwilling Latimer—remember that, however painful gradual cineration by fire may be, his death will produce unspeakable benefit to the public. From that moment no more fatal deference to the directors; no barbarous inattention to the anatomy and physiology of the human body, no commitment to the locomotive prison with warrant.—*Sidney Smith's "Letters."*

I cannot like all people alike. I have been trying all my life to like Scotchmen, and am obliged to desist from the experiment in despair. They cannot like me, and, in truth, I never knew one of that nation who attempted to do it. We know one another at first sight. There is an order of imperfect intellects, under which mine must be content to rank, which in its constitution is essentially anti-Caledonian. The brain of a true Caledonian is constituted upon quite a different plan. You cannot cry halves to anything that he finds. You must speak upon the square with him. He stops a metaphor like a suspected person in an enemy's country. I was present not long since, at a party of North Britons, where a son of Burns was expected, and happened to drop a silly expression, that I wished it were the father instead of the son, when four of them started up at once to inform me that that was impossible, because he was dead.—*Lamb's "Essays of Elia."*

There are two opposite ways by which some men make a figure in the world; one, by talking faster than they think, and the other, by holding their tongues and not thinking at all. By the first, many a smatterer acquires the reputation of a man of quick parts; by the other, many a dunderpate like the owl, comes to be considered the very type of wisdom. This, by-the-way, is a casual remark which I would not for the universe have it thought I apply to Governor Van Twiller. It is true he was a man shut up within himself, like an oyster, and rarely spoke except in monosyllables. If a joke were uttered in his presence, it was observed to throw him into a state of perplexity. When, after much explanation, the joke was made as plain as a pikestaff, he would exclaim, "Well, I see nothing in all that to laugh about." He was exactly five feet six inches in height and six feet five inches in circumference. His body was oblong and particularly capacious at bottom. His face presented a vast expanse, unfurrowed by any of those lines and angles which disfigure the countenance with what is termed expression.—*Irving's "Knickerbocker."*

"The opinion of these other branches of my family," pursued Mrs. Micawber, "is, that Mr. Micawber should immediately turn his attention to coal." "To what, ma'am?" "To coal," said Mrs. Micawber. "To the coal trade. Mr. Micawber was induced to think, on inquiry, that there might be an opening for a man of his talent in the Medway Coal Trade.

Then, as Mr. Micawber very properly said, the first step to be taken clearly was, to come and see the Medway. Which we came and saw. I say, we, Master Copperfield; for I never will," said Mrs. Micawber with emotion, "I never will desert Mr. Micawber." I murmured my admiration and approbation. "We came," repeated Mrs. Micawber, "and saw the Medway. My opinion of the coal trade on that river is, that it may require talent, but that it certainly requires capital. Talent, Mr. Micawber has; capital, Mr. Micawber has not.—*Dickens' "David Copperfield."*

CHAPTER IX.

MATTHEW ARNOLD'S ENGLISH STYLE.*

WHATEVER independent conclusions any one may have reached as to the writings and style of Matthew Arnold, it must be conceded that he is a commanding presence in English Letters. A poet of no inferior mould; a painstaking observer of the methods of modern education; a literary critic of acknowledged ability, and a writer of English prose as prominent, at present, as any of his English or American contemporaries, his work as an author demands examination, and will well repay any conscientious study that may be given it. In the chapter before us, it is with Mr. Arnold exclusively as a prose writer that we have to do, while, within the province of prose itself, we are to confine attention to the question of style, as dis-

* In connection with the English Style of Mr. Arnold and Mr. Emerson as here presented, the reader is referred to the author's "English Prose and Prose Writers," to such examples as Bacon, De Quincey, Burke and Lamb for pertinent illustrations of the various types of style under discussion.

tinct from any related question of personal character or opinion. It is not with our author's religious views as sound or unsound; nor with his views of education, politics, and social economy, that we are to deal; but with Mr. Arnold the man of letters. As far as the different divisions of his prose are concerned, they may be said to be theological, as seen in "St. Paul and Protestantism," "God and the Bible," "Literature and Dogma," "Last Essays on the Church and Religion;" educational, as seen in "Schools and Universities of the Continent," "Higher Schools and Universities in Germany," "Popular Education in France;" literary, as seen in "Essays in Criticism," "Culture and Anarchy," "Study of Celtic Literature," and "Addresses in America." These various discussions, shorter or longer, make up, with slight exceptions, the body of his published prose, and afford us an inviting field for the special survey of his work as a writer.

I. We note, at the outset, its *classical* character. The term classical, in this connection, may be used either in its more *specific*, technical sense, or in its more *enlarged* and current sense. If by it we mean the style of the old pagan authors in the best days of Greek and Roman letters, the word is eminently applicable to Mr. Arnold's writings. Most especially, it applies, in his case, to Grecian letters. In such an essay as "Literature and Science," we can clearly see the profound attachment of the author to anything Athenian, to the Attic order of expression, and to this, mainly, because of its beauty and grace. It has that "high symmetry" of form and method to which all later nations, as he argues, can hope but to approximate. That "instinct for beauty" which is common to the race will not only hold, as he affirms, the Greek language and literature in its historic place of prominence among liberal studies, but will make the imitation of its models an essential study with every patron of humane letters and verbal expression. It is a pleasing incident to note, that an edition of "Thucydides," by Dr. Thomas Arnold, evinces this same devotedness to the Greek, and thereby connects the scholarly instincts of the son with those of the father. Mr. Arnold thus insists in referring himself and his readers to the authors of antiquity. He is content to apply to prose what he has so emphatically applied to poetry, as he says: "In the sincere endeavor to learn and practise what is sound and true in poetical art, I seemed to myself to find the only sure guidance among the ancients." So conspicuons is this element of ancientness in his prose style, that it is only the reader of classical training and tastes who can best appreciate its meaning.

If we accept the word classical in its wider sense of *standard*, it is still, to a good degree, applicable to the prose before us. In his essay on "The Literary Influence of Academies," the author himself constantly employs the word in this generally-understood sense, of that which is idiomatic and unprovincial. In commenting on the style of Bossuet, he gives us, in one of his unique phrases, the clearest idea of classical prose as, "the prose of the centre." It is from this point of view that he rebukes Burke and other English essayists, in that they too often depart from the "centre," from what might be called, metropolitan English. Their style is suburban, and, to this degree, out of harmony with the governing spirit of the time. Where others fail, in this respect, Mr. Arnold substantially succeeds, and may be said to write an order of English which, with all its deference to pagan models, is the accepted English of modern England. In each of these senses, therefore, the style before us is classical. It is, in a word, a literary style, as distinct from being philosophic or scientific or even local. No English author of note, now living, is more distinctly a *littérateur* than was Mr. Arnold; more literary in his instincts, methods, habits, and aims. He was an author by profession and by preference. We have spoken of his essays as theological, educational, and literary. Such a classification is for convenience only. All his writings are literary more than they are anything else, and leave upon the reader the impression of the author's unqualified devotion to this particular type of expression.

If we inquire more particularly as to the chief *elements* of style included in the term classical, we may indicate them as *clearness* and *finish*. In a well-understood use of words, Mr. Arnold may be called a clear writer; substantially so in the conception of his ideas and in their communication to others. Every reader of his prose will recall the emphatic manner in which he gives to this quality the first place, as it deserves, in all literary work. He agreed with the old Welshman, Gerald de Barri, "that it is better to be dumb than not to be understood." He wrote all his books, as he wrote "Literature and Dogma," for a "better apprehension" of the subject in hand. He was constantly insisting on "lucidity," and thoroughly believed in it as a "character of perfection" in authorship.

When it is said that Mr. Arnold is a clear writer, this is not to say that he is clear in the same sense in which all other intelligible writers are clear, or that he is similarly clear on all subjects. With rare exceptions, however, he is practically intelligible on subjects capable of being made so, and to intelligent minds disposed to give to his writings a fair degree of thoughtful attention. When Mr. Arnold speaks of "the stream of tendency;" of "the Eternal, not ourselves, that makes for righteousness;" of "righteousness as salvation verifiably;" of the "criticism of life;" and of conduct as "three-fourths of life," we are simply to hold our objections in abeyance until he "comes to himself" and makes us understand his meaning, because he understands it himself. In such vague deliverances as these, we must remember that Mr. Arnold is not at his best, or even at his average of clearness as a writer. So true is this, that he is often seen to pass to the opposite extreme of *over-clearness*, to an undue repetition of idea and word, until the reader's patience is wearied and his intelligence insulted. Few of our author's admirers have failed to note this blemish, and deplore it. In all this, Mr. Arnold is consistent, and aims thereby to apply a principle which he approvingly quotes from Joubert: "It is by means of familiar words that style takes hold of the reader." Familiar words are not, however, repetitious. The logical elaboration of an idea is not, necessarily, its frequent re-statement. If we examine such an essay as "Culture and Anarchy" or "Literature and Science," with this particular error in mind, surprise will grow into repugnance at the injudicious recurrence of such phrases as "Sweetness and Light;" "the sense in us for conduct;" "the sense in us for beauty."

The "long sweep" which the author, in his essay on "Numbers," confesses he has taken in arriving at the point, is a sweep of fifty-six pages, in an article of seventy-one. Clear, beyond a question, this style is, but a little more of that "pregnant conciseness" for which he justly praised Milton, would have been in place, and made a style already intelligible still more decidedly so.

As to the author's style in the line of classical *finish*, scarcely too much of praise can be said. We come in contact here with the very essence of Mr. Arnold's personality,—his supreme devotion to literary form as an art, to the artistic or æsthetic side of authorship. Here, again, we find the explanation of his love of Greek letters. He loves them because they are, to his mind, the best human embodiment of the beautiful in language. For this reason, if for no other, he is at home in Athens and with Plato. Hence, his preference of Hellenism to Hebraism ; of beauty to sublimity ; of sentiment to action. The real Renaissance is to him but the reproduction of this old Attic art ; of that "genius and instinct for style" which he finds among the classic authors. Happily for the author, his antecedents and surroundings strongly contributed to this ruling principle. It was a part of his inheritance from his more distinguished father. His training at Rugby and Winchester and Oxford deepened and enlarged it. As professor of poetry at Oxford, he had studied and explained the governing laws of beauty ; as a writer of poetry, he had illustrated and applied them ; while, in the more didactic department of prose discourse, he ever evinced the presence of this "sense of beauty," and justified the appellation of "the apostle of culture." This he defines to be "a study and pursuit of perfection" ; a "passion for perfection" ; the final aim of the expression of thought. In choice of word, in structure of phrase and sentence, in unity and symmetry of outline, and in the general procedure of his work, this desire to reach the most consummate excellence of form is a dominant one. If the style is classically clear, it is, even more so, classically finished, and thus made attractive to the most fastidious taste. In this passionate devotion to the structural side of style, there is a danger lurking, and a danger, we are bound to add, which Mr. Arnold has not always escaped. There is here, at times, an *over-finish*, a finish for its own sake.

Mainly and generally, the style is clear and finished, and, in this sense, classical—a type of prose, partly, the result of his constant communion with Greek and French authors; partly, the result of English training: but, mainly, the result of that inborn "passion for perfection" which goes far to commend to the judgment and taste of cultured readers whatever he was pleased to pen.

II. We have spoken of Mr. Arnold as, above all else, an exponent of literary style. His style may also justly be termed *critical* and *controversial*. All his essays might well be called "Essays in Criticism." In his excellent paper on "The Function of Criticism," he gives us the general literary principles which, as he conceived them, lie at the basis of all literary judgment, and is willing, as an author, to be tested by them. Criticism he defines to be "a disinterested endeavor to learn and propagate the best that is known and thought in the world." That with which the literary censor has specially to do, is the "criticism of life." If we ask what, in Mr. Arnold's view, the chief conditions of successful criticism are, we find them to consist mainly in *knowledge* and *insight*. In addition to a large acquaintance with the comprehensive province of letters, there must be that delicacy of literary perception which is above all formal statute, though not unfriendly to it, and which fulfils, in the critic's personality, the practical function of intuitive judgment. No criticism, he would teach us, is worthy of the name, in which instinct is not greater than logical process; in which quickness of apprehension is not greater than mere acquisition, and where any decision is not known to be valid chiefly because it is seen and felt to be such. The critic, as he adds, is he who "has the faculty of judging with all the powers of his mind and soul at work together." He is the man in his mental and moral entirety absorbed, for the time, in the examination of authorship.

Hence it is that Mr. Arnold has done an invaluable work in minimizing the distance between creation and criticism in literature. Conceding, as he must have done, that the faculty of judging is of lower rank than the purely productive power, he still insists upon magnifying above its present status the judicial function. He sharply rebukes his favorite Wordsworth for taking so low a view of the critical art; illustrates the principle he is defending by a reference to Göethe, and is especially severe against that mercenary view of criticism by which it is reduced to the level of the merely practical. Not only is it, in Mr. Arnold's opinion, a high intellectual art, but it is based, also, on ethical principles and applied to ethical ends. Its purpose is "to see the object really as it is." It is to be prosecuted in that "justness of spirit" of which he so often speaks as essential to men of letters.

We have spoken of literary insight as seen in Mr. Arnold's critical style. This is most apparent by the way in which he subordinates facts to principles, and carefully elaborates these principles for the benefit of his readers. As he tells us, "Fineness and delicacy of perception to deal with the facts is the principal thing." Hence we find, in the prose before us, definite literary *principia* for the guidance of the novice. They read, by way of specimen, as follows: "The grand power of poetry is its interpretative power." "To ascertain the master current in the literature of an epoch is one of the critic's highest functions." "The thing to know of a writer is, where he is all himself and his best self; where he gives us what no other man gives us." Such are a few of these critical canons; passages that reveal genuine literary sagacity, and which, if applied to criticism in general, would exalt it at once to a scientific pursuit, worthy of the best endeavor of gifted men.

Reference has been made to the style in question as controversial. All criticism must be, to some extent, of this polemic character. This is not to say, however, that it is censorious. Though our author, as we shall see, has his faults as a critic, they are not here. We must accredit him with what he claims, "a disinterested endeavor," and confess that he brings conscience, as well as culture, to his work. There is manifest in his style a love of argument, a growing fondness, perhaps, for discussion, and yet very rarely present for any other reason than for ingenuous difference of opinion, and to defend what he conceives to be a radical literary law. The nature of the topics with which the author has dealt, the men and institutions with which he has been conversant, the age in which he has lived, made it impossible that he could have been critical without being controversial, That his critical style has not been more acrid than it has been, is largely due to the high ideal that he has always had of his art, and partly due to that scholarly equanimity of temper which is his, alike by constitution and training.

Thus much in praise of Mr. Arnold's critical style, and we turn, perforce, to what we must regard as his fundamental fault—its *dogmatic spirit.* Where this does not lead him into open contradictions, it gives to his writing a temper quite out of keeping with his clearly-pronounced views. Though this dogmatism is apparent in all his prose, it is least so in that which is educational; most so, in that which is theological; while far too conspicuous in that which is mainly literary. No man has opposed the dogmatic tone more than he, and yet he is, here, among the chief of sinners. The author of "Literature and Dogma" knew what was meant by each of these terms. We are speaking now of the inner spirit of style, and not at all of the subject-matter as expressed in opinion or belief. Independence of judgment is one thing; bold independence of the judgment of others is a different and a more dangerous thing. Even a genius in criticism must take account of the conclusions of others, and, at times, wait upon their word. What may be called the indifferent tone of Mr. Arnold's critical style is in keeping with this dogmatism, if not, indeed, a part of it. The critic is thoroughly satisfied with himself. One of his favorite words is, Sweetness. Who would be so daring as to charge our author with its manifestation! What he calls "urbanity" is but another name for cautious reserve, an unsympathetic reticence which often becomes cynical. We are not sure but that this aristocratic manner was more and more apparent in Mr. Arnold, and never more pronounced than in his latest utterances. Despite his well-meaning theories, the appellation given him of an "æsthetic reformer" is not quite undeserved. In the face of his avowed devotion to the middle classes, his references to their "hardness and vulgarity and grotesque illusions" is not the best way to conciliate the Philistines. Full of schemes for the people's good, the mere mention of the name of John Bright, the people's practical friend, was enough to stir within him the "scorn of scorn," and drive his pen to the verge of personality. A son of Oxford, he was devoted to its "faith and traditions," and preferred to appear as a representative of the "Remnant," the acknowledged apostle of classical restraint. Criticism has, at its best, quite enough of this unfeeling element in it, this urban indifference to the outside. To our own mind, the one most repellant feature of this distinguished writer is this imperial pompousness, this air of self-assertion, which amounts, at times, to nothing short of a literary strut. The world is too old and too wise for such posing as this, and it is well for all to know it. It is the most natural thing imaginable for a critical style to become self-assertive, and yet the intelligent classes are tired of it, and are looking for more humility at the seat of judgment. Mr. Arnold is regarded by some as an erratic guide in criticism. The opinion is not without basis, in so far as the error in question is present. In his several addresses recently delivered in America, we note most suggestive examples of this parade of parts—this literary *hauteur*. The dogmatic temper apart, however, Mr. Arnold's prose writings exhibit the better features of the critical style. They are the product of a man of large literary acquisition, of high classical taste, of a marked degree of literary acumen and of ingenuous literary motive, and must take their place among the representative criticisms of the time.

III. To our mind, one of the chief characteristics of a good book and a good style is, that it is *suggestive* and *stimulating*, that it has in it intellectual *vitality* a deep under-current of thought and life far below all that is visible, and giving to what we term expression its vivifying and effective force. Mr. Stedman speaks of Mr. Arnold as a "poet of the intellect." The appellation is in place relative to his prose. He generally gives us something that has cost him thought, and which is fitted thereby to awaken thought within us. How could a son of Dr. Thomas Arnold have failed to exhibit a masculine vigor of mind? There is in the style a kind of Gothic robustness, through the influence of which it impresses itself upon the reader, and infuses into his being something of this same Teutonic spirit. Mr. Arnold had been, from his earliest intellectual life, an observer and inquirer, a reader and student and thinker. He had what he himself would call, "a scientific passion" for knowledge and for its communication to others. We have referred to a division of his prose works as educational. It is just to affirm that his style throughout has this educational and educating quality; that didactic character for which he so admired the poetry of Wordsworth. In the words of Montesquieu, it seeks "to render an intelligent being still more intelligent," and, in the truly Baconian spirit, to add somewhat to the sum of human truth. Our author, in commenting on the character of Burke, remarks "that he was so great because he brought thought to bear on politics." It is one of the most helpful services rendered by

Mr. Arnold that he has brought thought to bear on literature and style, lifting them from the low plane on which the French school of his day had placed them, and coördinating them with all the invigorating branches of mental life. "Let men say what they please," he writes, "if what they please to say is worth saying." He would endorse the sentiment of George Eliot in "Theophrastus Such": "Blessed is the man who, having nothing to say, abstains from giving us wordy evidence of the fact." Behind the word, as he holds, is the idea; behind the style is the subject-matter, and nothing is gained by any writer in substituting mere vocabulary for sense. The style is thus instructive and incitive. It often implies more than it fully unfolds, and serves to quicken within the reader a genuine literary impulse. It is the intellectual style as we have discussed it.

No one can read the prose of Mr. Arnold with carefulness and sympathetic attention, without becoming a wiser man, and without having awakened within him a desire to become even wiser still, along the lines of inquiry opened up before him by the author. His style has thus always been attractive to the intelligent classes of every community, to the well-bred and well-read. Among university and college men, Mr. Arnold has always found devoted admirers; not so much because he has written largely on university topics, but because he has written on most topics in the university manner. It is this intellectual element of style which, after all, is its distinctive element, on the basis of which the prose we are examining may safely be commended to the thoughtful young men of the land. It will be an auspicious omen in our literary history, and of untold advantage to our college men, when such an order of reading as this will quite displace the miscellaneous literature of the hour, and those books be most eagerly sought which are the fullest of mental content.

We are speaking exclusively of our author's style, and not of his individual beliefs, when we thus emphasize .the excellence of his prose as a vigorous protest against all that is superficial. Few of us cannot but regret that Mr. Arnold has not confined himself more closely to strictly literary themes, of which he is an accredited master, and has essayed so frequently to play the part of a doctrinal disputant in regions of inquiry where, in thought and style, he has appeared at his worst. Though Principal Fairbairn and others have called attention to the vogue into which Mr. Arnold's theological writings have come, we cannot but rejoice that his "Last Essays on the Church and Religion" were, indeed, the last on such a line of topics, and that his attention was more discreetly directed to essays on criticism and culture. Within his proper sphere, he is unique and able, so as to have become, at the time of his premature death, a conspicuous exponent of modern thought as expressed in modern literature. His "Posthumous Essays" confirm such a view.

In speaking thus of our author's legitimate province as a thinker and writer, we are led to mark what we must regard as the mental *narrowness* of his outlook. Mr. Stedman has called our attention to the "limitations" of Mr. Arnold's poetic power, his want of "lightness of touch" and of "range of affections." In the study of his prose, we may consistently speak of the limitation of his intellectual range. His reach of mind, at the farthest, was restricted. In his vision of truth, at the longest, he was somewhat near-sighted, and failed to cover that spacious area of inquiry which it is the prerogative of genius to compass. We shall probably encounter, at this point, the decided opposition of many of our readers, or, at least, be told that, if the mental breadth of our author's style is an open question at all, he must have the benefit of the doubt. We hold, however, to the assertion made, and hold it as fully accordant with all that has been said by way of praise as to the clearness, finish, critical perception, and general intellectual suggestiveness of his style. These are all possible features apart from great breadth of mental vision, while the over-clearness and over-culture and dogmatic assertion to which we have referred, are proof in point of this very limitation of faculty.

Mr. Arnold's style is not, in the fullest sense of the words, philosophic, far-reaching, and catholic. Though not superficial, it is not profound; and while contributing, as far it goes, to genuine mental impulse, it has not that "mental stretch" in it which marks the seer. As already stated, Mr. Arnold was a man of letters, a student of style, a literary critic. He has said, perhaps, more than he meant to say, when he wrote in "Literature and Dogma:" "For the good of letters is that they require no extraordinary acuteness, such as is required to handle the theory of causation, and letters, therefore, meet in us a greater want than does logic." True or false, this is the author's view of the mental requisition of letters as a branch of liberal learning, and is the view which his prose illustrates. The central word of his vocabulary is culture, and though he defines it to be "an harmonious expansion of all the powers," it is strikingly apparent that the expansion is but partial. In this respect, at least, the great Master of Rugby is his superior, in that wide-eyed view of thought and life that takes in everything within the visible horizon, and even peers beyond it.

Here, as we believe, lies the main explanation of the fact that Mr. Arnold, in his prose, is an *essayist*, and nothing more. Whatever the particular form in which his writings are published, their original form was that of the essay or dissertation, as distinct from the book proper, with its exhaustive discussion of the subject in hand. Conceding to the essay all that has historically been claimed for it, or that can legitimately be given it, it is not the book proper, any more than one of Milton's sonnets is to be classified as a lyric with "Comus," or than an heroic ode, such as, "Alexander's Feast," is an epic. This is not mainly because the one is briefer than the other, but because they differ in mental grasp and procedure, as also in spirit and purpose. Burns wrote as genuine poetry as was ever written by any son of song. He had not the poetic breadth, however, to construct an epic. Wordsworth, intellectual as he was, had not this epic faculty. Lord Bacon was an essayist, but he was transcendently more. Addison, in prose, was an essayist only, and the difference in the mental girth of these two writers will mark the difference between range and restriction. The style of Mr. Arnold's prose is intellectual, but not in the Baconian sense; while, even within the limited province of the essay itself, such a writer as De Quincey is his undoubted superior. Though his style does not reveal a man of one idea, it does reveal a man of a comparatively limited number of ideas, which, at times, he reiterates, as he does his words, slightly to our distaste. The process of condensation applied with "executive severity" to his writings would materially reduce their volume and enhance their value. All this conceded, we repeat our assertion as to the general stimulus of his style, within the range of reflection and observation that he may be said to occupy. When fully at home with the subject in hand, what he knows, he knows clearly; what he writes, he writes in classical English, and the reading is mentally salutary. A genius neither in verse nor prose, he has yet, as Mr. Stedman intimates, accomplished, in some of his verse, the substantial results of genius, and has often, we may add, accomplished them in prose.

IV. We are now brought to what may be regarded as the most interesting feature of the style before us—its distinctive *moral gravity*. Critics of his poetry have quite agreed in placing him in "the contemplative group" of poets, in that moralistic school of writers which is so conspicuous in English letters. Our author himself tells us that by authorship "the moral fibre must be braced," and holds it as essential to all literary criticism that the ethical element must be acknowledged. Attention has been called to the æsthetic beauty of Mr. Arnold's prose, especially as it is dependent on a careful study of Greek models. This literary sedateness, however, is Roman in its type, a kind of Senecan sobriety of demeanor which is in fullest keeping with the author's personality. Even in his poetry, we mark the prevalence of the graver themes, as "Balder Dead" and "Thyrsis," while the explanation of his comparative failure in the treatment of lighter topics is found in this adaptation of his mind to the more serious aspects of truth. There is in Matthew Arnold's authorship but little, if any, light literature. That he should have attempted the production of a romance is quite unthinkable. He quotes with fervent approbation the pungent words of Joubert as to "the monstrosities of fiction"—that "they have no place in literature." "They who produce them are not really men of letters." His distinctively theological essays are an evidence of this subjective habit of mind. He has a kind of "devout energy" that leads him into the region of religious inquiry. Though his prose is not without satire, the satire itself is of the more serious order, after the manner of Juvenal rather than that of Swift. How notable the absence of wit and humor, as they appear in Addison and Lamb! How direct and literal the phraseology! How devoid of playful pleasantry, as it soberly proceeds to unfold its meaning toward a definite result! As in his verse, when the dramatic is attempted, it is on the side of the tragic rather than the comic, so in his prose, this magisterial sedateness is the dominant spirit, and serves to exclude the trivial and belittling. Mr. Arnold has called the style of Homer "eminently noble." There is this quality of Homeric nobleness in his own style; a kind of classical dignity of address that gives it an attractiveness to every reflective reader. Partly, a product of inherited character, partly, the result of personal temperament, and, partly, the expression of culture, it must receive a valid place in any proper estimate of his style.

If we inquire as to the special type of this literary gravity, we find it to be *ethical* rather than religious, Hellenic rather than Hebraic. It is best described in the author's own language, as "intellectual seriousness." If we compare, at this point, the father and the son, we clearly see the difference between the deep religious spirit of the one and the ethical propriety of the other. It is the difference between piety proper and external moral decorum; between Milton and Macaulay. The radical, biblical sense of the word spiritual, as used by Thomas Arnold, is gradually modified by the son, until we reach what is called æsthetic symmetry of character, a faculty for discerning the true, the beautiful, and the good, wherever present. To resist the devil, meant with the father what it meant with Paul and Bunyan. With the son, it meant the opposition of the soul to all degrading tendencies, the enthronement of Beauty over the Beast. In a word, Mr. Arnold's style is serious in the sense of being ethically correct and earnest, and this is all.

Just here we are prepared to note what we are obliged to call the *despondent* tone of Mr. Arnold's style. He is, in no true sense, a cheerful, hearty, whole-souled English writer, as Scott and Thackeray and Christopher North may be said to be. The cast of the prose is Carlylean, and strongly impressed with the influence of Göethe. Students of Mr. Arnold's poetry must be well aware of this undertone of sadness that runs like a sombre current below the visible level of his verse. Herein is one of those limitations of his poetic genius, whereby the spontaneity of his style is impaired, and the head waits not upon the heart. We cannot, therefore, expect to find in his poems free flexibility of movement, blitheness and buoyancy of spirit, and the impulse of deep emotion, in that the nature from which such poetic fruits are "furnished forth" is wanting. So is it in his prose. Seriousness is too often seen to give place to sadness, and to a sadness which is nothing less than Byronic and oppressive. Of the presence and the pressure of this weight upon him, Mr. Arnold himself is not always aware. There is a something in the sentence and the line—he scarcely knows what—that binds it to the earth and prevents its free excursion heavenward. In this profitless effort to lift the world from its lower tendencies by culture only; in this pursuit of perfection through imperfect agencies; in this almost cruel restriction of the spirit within the circle of the humanities; in this well-meant but unwise attempt to eliminate the supernatural from the problem of life,—in this, indeed, we have the fact of sadness and its sufficient explanation. The "sick fatigue and languid doubt," which the author himself deplores, will never give place to that "sweet calm" of mind that he so craves, until the established relation of things is accepted, and Christianity takes rank above culture. This feature apart, the prose is marked by a solid and impressive earnestness, which never tolerates the trifling, and is an order of prose especially timely in an age inclined so strongly as this to the frivolous in authorship. In this respect, if not so in others, Mr. Arnold's style is Baconian and Miltonic, never descending to the plane of the charlatan for the sake of effect, but ever keeping aloft on the high table-land of thought and motive, among the sober-minded contributors to the cause of good letters.

If asked, as we close, what is the most useful service that Mr. Arnold has rendered, in his style, to modern England and America, we answer, the wide diffusion of the *literary spirit*, the emphasis of literature as a most important department of education and an essential factor in all national progress. This result he has accomplished, in part, by his unwearied exaltation of the mental above the merely material, and, in part, by his earnest endeavor to stimulate the people to the attainment of that culture which to him is the crowning principle of all literature and life. Nothing is more needed among the English-speaking peoples of to-day than the free circulation of this literary life. Despite such high literary antecedents and traditions, and the goodly number of English authors steadily at work along the old literary lines, so strong is the "stream of tendency" in the direction of commercialism, that special effort is needed to prevent its influx even into the centres of intellectual culture. This tendency is even more marked in what Mr. Emerson has called "this great, intelligent, sensual, and avaricious America."

If we inquire further into the extent and probable *permanence* of Mr. Arnold's influence as a prose writer, we must answer, first of all, that he cannot be consistently called a popular English essayist. There is not enough of the common or colloquial element in the style to give it currency among the great body of what he terms the middle class. That extreme æstheticism to which we have referred, as also his dogmatic independence and indifference of manner, would serve to narrow the circle of appreciative readers, while, even among the higher classes themselves, our author is read by many who read only to dissent. If we compare his essays, in this respect, with those of Lamb and Macaulay, the difference is marked in favor of the latter, and the difference is one between restricted and general circulation.

Mr. Arnold cannot be said to have formed a *school*, either in prose or verse. Whatever his constituency may be, they do not stand related to him as an organic body to an acknowledged leader, accepting his literary dicta without question, and devoting their energies to the dissemination of his teachings. Young men, especially, who, at first, are attacted to his style and committed to it as an unerring guide, come, at length, in their maturer judgment, to question where they have blindly accepted, and somewhat modify their allegiance. Mr. Arnold, in his "American Addresses," refused to rank Mr. Emerson, as he also did Mr. Carlyle, among "the great writers" or "the great men of letters." He used the word "great" as it is applicable to such historic authors as Plato and Cicero, Pascal and Voltaire and Bacon—writers "whose prose, by a kind of native necessity, is true and sound," who have "a genius and an instinct for style." From such a "charmed circle" as this, Mr Arnold himself must be excluded. A representative writer of English prose, he is not so in the largest sense, as Cicero, in Latin letters, or De Quincey, in English. Whatever the merits of his style may be, as we have discussed them, he has not that "vision and faculty divine" which belongs to the eminently great prose-writer as to the eminently great poet. He does not see deep enough and far enough to pen oracular words for those who are waiting for them. Culture, as he conceived it, can never rise to the height of power. Criticism, as he applied it, can never be more than an elegant art; while style itself, as he illustrated it, can never be that inspiring procedure which we find it to be in the writings of the masters—in the poetry of Shakespeare or in the prose of Pascal. A cultured, an acute, and a dignified style is one thing, and marks the good writer. A profound, philosophic, comprehensive, and soul-stirring style is another and a grander thing, and marks the 'great writer." We have a style before us that pleases our taste, impresses our minds, corrects, in many instances, our erroneous judgments, and rebukes our natural tendencies to the lighter and baser forms of literature; and this is all. When the profoundest depths of our being are to be reached and roused; when we are to be uplifted to that sublime spiritual out-look of which Milton and Longinus speak; when we are to be so addressed and moved that the thoughts of the author take possession of us, and make us efficient factors in the world's intellectual and moral advancement, then must we look elsewhere than here,—to those supremely-gifted authors who are great of a truth, and who make us great as well, to the degree in which we hold reverential converse with them. That style is great, and that only, which is instinct throughout with the very spirit of power; which, while obedient to the laws of literary art, is immeasurably above all art; and, with all its marks of human origin and limitation about it, is seen to have, in its character and method, something that is supernal.

MATTHEW ARNOLD'S STYLE.

Examples.

It is impossible to rise from reading Epictetus or Marcus Aurelius, without a sense of constraint and melancholy, without feeling that the burden laid upon man is well nigh greater than he can bear. Honor to the sages who have felt this and, yet, have borne it! The paramount virtue of religion is, that it has lightened up morality; that it has supplied the emotion and inspiration needful for carrying the sage along the narrow way perfectly, for carrying the ordinary man along it at all. Even the religions with most dross in them have had something of this virtue; but the Christian religion manifests it with unexampled splendor.—"*Essays in Criticism.*"

Oxford, the Oxford of the past, has many faults, and she has heavily paid for them in defeat, in isolation, in want of hold upon the modern world. Yet we in Oxford. . . . have not failed to seize one truth—the truth that beauty and sweetness are essential characters of a complete human perfection. When I insist on this I am all in the faith and tradition of Oxford. I say boldly that this our sentiment for beauty and sweetness. . . . has been at the bottom of our attachment to so many beaten causes, of our opposition to so many triumphant movements. . . . We have not won our political battles, we have not carried our main points; we have not stopped our adversaries' advice. . . . but we have told silently upon the mind of the country. . . . we have kept up our own communications with the future. . . .—"*Culture and Anarchy.*"

The great men of culture are those who have had a passion for diffusing, for making prevail, for carrying from one end of society to the other, the best ideas of their time. Such a man was Abelard. Such were Lessing and Herder in Germany, at the end of the last century, and their services were inestimably precious. Because they humanized knowledge; because they broadened the basis of life and intelligence; because they worked powerfully. . . . to make reason and the will of God prevail.—"*Essays.*"

And therefore, to say the truth, I cannot really think that humane letters are in much actual danger from being thrust out from their leading place in education. So long as human nature is what it is, their attractions will remain irresistible. As with Greek, so with letters generally; they will some day come, we may hope, to be studied more rationally, but they will not lose their place. . . . If they lose it for a time, they will get it back again. We shall be brought back to them by our wants and aspirations. . . . The majority of men will always require humane letters, and so much the more, as they have the greater results of science to relate to the need in man for conduct and to the need in him for beauty.—"*Discourses in America.*"

CHAPTE

EMERSON'S ENGLISH STYLE.

MR. EMERSON, all counter-criticism conceded, is one of America's foremost men—a prominent presence in our history and authorship; one of those representative men, as he himself has called them, who go far to give permanent renown to a nation and raise it immeasurably above mediocrity.

Despite all conflict of opinion as to his ability and work, his name must be placed in the list of great names, and an earnest protest expressed against that narrowness of view which would presume to call him "a charlatan and sciolist."

In the discussion of English Style, we are not to deal directly with Mr. Emerson's personal character, but with it only so far as it enters vitally into his work as an author. In the pages of Conway and Cabot, Motley and Ireland, Cooke and Holmes, there may be found all that is needed in the line of biography. Nor can there be discussed, save incidentally, his philosophic and religious views; his own language, at this point, being sufficiently conclusive, as he says—"I prefer to be called a Christian theist." It is with Emerson the author and the writer that the literary student has to do, and, even here, he must confine himself to the department of his prose writings as distinct from his poetry. The study in hand is a study of style, and the question to be answered is the important and somewhat difficult one—What are the salient characteristics of Mr. Emerson's English style, or the style, Emersonian.

I. First, and most significant, is its Intellectuality. It is in no sense contradictory, but highly consistent and logical, as has been shown, to speak of an intellectual style, marked by the dominance of subject matter over all that is external, and ever insisting upon the truth that language is the expression of thought, for the sake, primarily, of the thought itself. When Mr. Arnold, in his "American Addresses," denies Mr. Emerson the claim to being a high order of philosophic writer, the term philosophic is used in the specific, technical sense, and not in the wider sense of intellectual. The English critic is referring to his peculiar philosophical ideas and to that particular type of prose in which they are expressed. Mr. Emerson himself is constantly calling attention to this mental element in authorship, and cannot utter too much in its praise. "The effect of any writing on the public mind," he says, "is mathematically measurable by its depth of thought. How much water does it drain? If it awaken you to think; if it lift you from your feet . . . then the effect is to be wide and permanent."

It would be difficult for any one to study carefully the face of Emerson without detecting this higher quality. The very lineaments are intellectual, indicative of the seer and the oracle; vatic and prophetic in their outline; fully answering to those descriptions of facial expressiveness which Mrs. Browning gives us in her, "Vision of Poets," as she sings so sublimely of Shakespeare and Æschylus, Sophocles and Homer, Pindar, Sappho and Lucretius, Dante and Petrarch, and of the angel before the altar whose "brow's height was sovereign." "There are faces," says Emerson, "so fluid with expression, so flushed and rippled with the play of thought, that we can hardly find what the mere features really are."

Notice, further, the nature of the themes which our author discusses; such as "Intellect," "Plato," "The Philosophers," "Ability," "Originality," "Greatness," "Education," "The Scholar," and, so, on. The reader is, at once, impressed with their marked mentality. Even when not in themselves mental, they are mentally presented and applied. Critics have spoken rightly of the "solid value of his thoughts." It is for this reason that we may equally rightly speak of the solid value of his style. We are not surprised to read that for three successive years at Harvard he discoursed to the students on "The Natural History of the Intellect." Plato and Plutarch, Homer and Dante, Milton and Shakespeare were his ideals and favorites because they embodied the intellectual element in style and character. He speaks appreciatively of "Coleridge, as a catholic mind, hungry for ideas." Emerson was a thinker with pen in hand, a thoughtful writer—a writer full of thought; always cogitating; always mentally observing and inferring; always walking with uplifted spirit, but with bowed head, seeking to peer deeper and still deeper into the innermost heart of truth and things.

Some of the evidences of this intellectuality of style may be profitably noted.

1. Originality. We may call it, without modification, Genius. He did his own thinking, in his own way, courteously but absolutely regardless of the thinking of others. He could not have done otherwise had he wished. "Insist on yourself; never imitate," is his oft-repeated exhortation. "He is great who is what he is from nature, and who never reminds us of others." If he admires Plato and Shakespeare and the great ones of earth, it is, as Mr. Holmes expresses it, "always with a reservation." That reservation is his own individuality and his own individual opinion, which, despite all inducement and pressure, he will never surrender.

Among all his characteristic essays, none is more decidedly so than that on "Self-Reliance," filled to the full with this cardinal merit of personality, taking for its text the well-known affirmation—"To believe your own thought, to believe that what is true for you in your private heart is true for all men, that is genius. Speak your latent conviction, and it shall be the universal sense." To the divinity students at Cambridge he says, "It is not instruction, but provocation only that I can receive from another soul. What he announces, I must find true in *me* or reject."

Hence, conversant as Emerson was with books, he was their master, not their slave. If he writes on the subject of Quotation, the significant caption is—Quotation and Originality. "Books are the best things," he says, "well used; abused, among the worst. I had better never see a book than to be warped by its attraction, clean out of my own orbit." "Genius is always sufficiently the enemy of genius by over-influence. The English dramatic poets have Shakespearized for two hundred years." It is at this point of original, personal opinion in authorship that Emerson reminds us so forcibly of Carlyle, in whose character and teachings he found much of the affinity that he did, through the medium of their common independence of other thinkers.

2. Closely akin to this originality of view is, Vigor or Incisiveness of style—a mental weightiness of expression that is Baconian in its type and carries with it its own convincing efficacy.

To attempt to select from the pages of Emerson's "Essays" what we may call, passages of power, is simply invidious. The essays chosen at random are packed with potency. Any page, opened at a venture, will reveal this condensed forcefulness, mainly resulting from the thought behind it, *e. g.*, "A profound thought classifies all things; a profound thought will lift Olympus." "Go and talk with a man of genius, and the first word he utters sets all your so-called knowledge afloat and at large." "A man, a personal ascendency, is the only great phenomenon." "Each man has his own vocation. The talent is the call." "Let a man believe in God, and not in names and places and persons." "All language is vehicular and transitive, and is good, as ferries are, for conveyance; not as farms and houses are, for homestead." There is visible in these and kindred passages not only a vigor of intellect in the more didactic sense, but a vigor of soul. There is an intellectual passion in the words and lines, that gives them vitality, and, at times, thrilling impressiveness. The prose of Emerson, in this respect, throbs with life. The paragraphs pulsate as we read them. They are more than forcible. They are eloquent and emotive, and stir us to the quick of our characters and powers.

Special attention should here be called to Emerson's mental incisiveness as a writer, to that terse and telling way he has, which is all his own, of presenting and fixing the idea that he utters. "Give me health and a day, and I will make the pomp of emperors ridiculous." "The moment discourse rises above the ground-line of familiar facts and is inflamed with passion or exalted by thought, it clothes itself in images." "No man ever prayed heartily without learning something." "Only so much do I know as I have lived." "The main enterprise of the world for splendour, for extent, is the upbuilding of a man."

Not infrequently this incisive statement takes the form of *satire*, when Emerson gives us some of his most pithy and pungent sentences. His essays on Education, Character and Travel are full of this satiric element. His frequent references to American politics and parties; to charitable societies; to professional and civic fraud; to such visionary enterprises as Brook Farm, and to the modern tendency to extremes, furnish abundant evidence of this trenchant irony, and exhibit his mental vigor in a new and striking light. In fine, the style throughout is instinct with intellectual life. Original, vigorous, incisive and condensed, it is full of that "mental stuff" of which Lord Bacon speaks, and is, at times, almost overborne by its own weight of thought. Behind the sentence and the essay, we always discern the living personality, the thinking *ego*, and it is he who is talking with us, out of the lowest deeps of his consciousness.

Mr. Emerson had his faults as a thinker, but that he was a thinker none will question. As an intellectual author, he is, at times, open to adverse criticism, but that he was such an author cannot be rationally doubted. Not a scholar in the strictly professional and technical sense, there is an element in his writing which we must call scholarly. It is Platonic in that it is full of ideas, surcharged and suffused with thought, and makes us think and think again as we peruse it. The pages fairly bristle with reflections and intimations. There is more between the lines than in the lines. The style, throughout, is indicative and potential, and characterized by that "immense suggestiveness" which Whipple attributes to Shakespeare.

Before leaving the subject of Emerson's intellectual character as a writer, it remains to call attention to his radical defect in this direction. This defect may be expressed under various forms. We deem it best to call it—as the older English writers would have called it—Want of Logical Sequence,—the absence of a consecutive progress of reasoning and thinking. Though the theme discussed is always clear, and though, in most instances, the emphatic point of the discussion is clearly stated at the outset, the actual discussion itself is often desultory rather than logical. It is interesting to observe, that Emerson himself understood alike the prime importance of this law of order and his too frequent failure to exhibit and apply it. In his paper on "Eloquence,"—he writes —"Next to the knowledge of the fact and its law is method, which constitutes the genuis and efficiency of all remarkable men." "Is there method in your consciousness?" he asks. In answer to a letter from his friend Dr. Ware, he writes, "I have always been—from my very incapacity of methodical writing—a chartered libertine, lucky when I could make myself understood. I could not give an account of myself, if challenged." "Nothing is plainer," says Dr. Holmes, his appreciative biographer, "than that it was Emerson's calling to supply impulses and not methods." He is never at great pains to co-ordinate his thoughts. He makes no attempt to discover and constantly keep in the sight of himself and his reader the logical nexus by which truths and systems of truth are relatively adjusted. When Mr. Arnold speaks of him as "the propounder of a philosophy," he means to add, conversely, that he failed to elaborate and explain the philosophy he propounded.

It has been questioned, and plausibly, whether he ever designed to formulate, as a philosophical writer, a philosophical system. Certain it is, that he never did formulate such a system. Each idea, whatever its nature, stood by itself and for itself. If logically related to his other deliverances, precedent and subsequent, well; if not, equally well. "Here I sit," he says, "and read and write with very little system." Mr. Arnold, as a thinker and critic, is not slow, of course, to see the manifest weakness of Mr. Emerson's mental character at this point, as he says, "His arrangement of philosophical ideas has no progress; no evolution in it." It is to this lack of sequence that Carlyle more than once refers, in his familiar correspondence with Emerson. Hence, we find in these brilliant essays little that is analytical; in this sense, little that is Baconian.

It is safe to say that, in this view of it, Mr. Emerson's style, as his mind, is intuitional rather than reflective. There is a lack of what he himself has aptly called—"constructive energy;" a purposed subordination of consecutive argument to the individual instincts of the judgment and the reason. It would be difficult to conceive of him as following, on the basis of gathered facts, the slow processes of inductive reasoning from premises to conclusion. We look in vain throughout his essays for the statement of truth in syllogistic form. As Dr. Holmes tersely expresses it—"His gift was insight." What he could not see at once, he could not see at all, and, in the deep, intense action of his mind, had neither the patience nor power to hold himself bound to any scientific order of procedure. Emerson's mind and art were not so much illogical as unlogical. He was what Coleridge called "*non sequacious*." Hence, too much faith must not be placed in his conclusions as a critic, if, indeed, his avowals as to men and principles could justly take the name of conclusions. In this respect, he was Carlyle's inferior, who with all his errors and obliqulties, often reasoned his way along from step to step and reached results by gradational process.

Careful students of the writings and style of Emerson have called attention to his preference of miscellany to the more extended and exhaustive forms of topical discussion. The explanation is not far to find. His preference was here the exponent of his ability. His genius was in depth of penetration rather than in range of outlook. If we may so express it, his power was perpendicular; not lateral or linear. Though his themes covered the general area of truth, and may be said to have been well-nigh unlimited, his treatment of themes was limited, rarely evincing that many-sidedness of discussion which is the mark of the comprehensive writer. It is thus natural to find that within the sphere of English Prose, Emerson was confined to memoirs, sketches, orations and miscellany. How striking and, in a sense, plaintive is his remark to Carlyle, "I am the victim of miscellany." In speaking of Coleridge, he notes, "as the misfortune of his life, his vast attempts, but most inadequate performings." In the ten volumes of his prose writings, we meet with nothing save essays and addresses. Within this area he is a master, but seldom ventures beyond the bounds of it, even by way of relaxation.

All this admitted, however, in the line of limitation, we revert with interest and emphasis to the marked intellectuality of Emerson's style inside the province to which his powers assigned him and held him.

In the direction of what we may designate, a subjective English style, he was without a peer. His genius as a man and an author was introspective. He was ever descending to the centre and interior, and, when he spoke or wrote, there was a something subterranean in it all. "Look in thy heart and write," he says, quoting from the courtly Sidney. Style, he would tell us, is the revelation of the inner self, the expression of a man's intellectual personality upon the open page and, therefore, despite all its defects, must be original and potent.

II. Ethical Energy. Though we come to the discussion of this characteristic as second in order, it is by no means clear which is the more distinctive quality of Mr. Emerson's character and style—the intellectual or the ethical. We have spoken of the mental type of his face. Its moral significance is equally striking. No one could have looked upon the features of Emerson when living, as no one can now carefully study his portrait, apart from the impression of the *character* that was in him. There was what Mrs. Browning has called, "the forehead royal with the truth." There were "the lips and jaw, grand-made and strong, as Sinai's law." It is of "chosen men and women" that Emerson says—"Their face and manners carry a certain grandeur, like time and justice."

We may truly say, that his great, cardinal characteristic was *character*. He bore about with him in material life the salient marks of his clerical lineage and habit. Before and after he was "approbated to preach," in 1826, he was morally inclined thereto, while his surrender of the ministry on doctrinal grounds in no whit indicated a decrease of ethical spirit. We have spoken of the intellectual type of his themes. Their ethical quality is even more apparent, such as, "Literary Ethics," "Spiritual Laws," "The Over-Soul," "Character," "Montaigne the Sceptic," "Religion," "Worship," "Behaviour," "Inspiration," "Immortality," "The Preacher," and, above all, that masterpiece of morals, "The Sovereignty of Ethics," in which he speaks, in his inimitable way, "of the immense energy of the sentiment of duty and the awe of the supernatural." "Men are respectable only as they respect." "We delight in children because of that religious eye which belongs to them." Even where the topics themselves are not ethical, they are ethically discussed, and his final appeal, after all others have failed, is always to the deepest moral emotions and instincts.

There are some specific expressions of this quality of Emerson's style to which particular attention should be called.

1. We are impressed, at the outset, with the Sincerity of his style. We can say of him as he said of Thoreau—"He is sincerity itself." As has been well expressed, "No man who is himself sincere can doubt Emerson's sincerity." In thought, method, aim and general procedure, there is an attractive simplicity of type, often taking the form of a sweet and genial manner, —indicative of an innate graciousness of soul. "If a man dissemble," says Emerson, "he goes out

of acquaintance with his own being." "There are living organisms so transparent," writes Dr. Holmes, "that we can see their hearts beating and their blood flowing—so transparent was the life of Emerson." "When a man speaks the truth in the spirit of truth," he adds, "his eye is as clear as the heavens." "The way to speak and write what shall not go out of fashion is to speak and write sincerely."

2. Equally noticeable, as an ethical element, is the Sobriety of his work,—a matter with him of conscience and of taste, ancestral and connatural, an essential factor of his highest personality. There is in all he does and says that "intellectual seriousness" of which Mr. Arnold has spoken in other connections—that dignified serenity of spirit which is one of the infallible marks of the highest minds. It is under the potent influence of this central characteristic that he writes —"Out of our shallow and frivolous way of life, how can greatness ever grow?" "We spend our incomes for a hundred trifles and not for the things of a man." As Milton, before him, he had nothing to do with frivolities. "There was a majesty about him beyond all other men I have known," says Lowell, "and he dwelt, habitually, in that ampler and diviner air to which most of us, if ever, rise but occasionally." Even his humor is grave and decorous in its character—the more informal expression of that profound serenity of spirit which subdued all who came to his presence,

and which casts over the body of his authorship a kind of hallowed peace. He admired Milton and Dante, and the great Greek tragedians largely because of their personal and literary gravity.

We may advance a step further and note, that the ethical quality takes, at times, the form of Spirituality. There is the constant presence and exercise of the moral sense, a delicate and an unerring sensibility, such as we rarely find in authors.

His absorbing perusal of such writers as Augustine, Plato, Plutarch, and Jeremy Taylor was largely due to that spiritual affinity that existed between his soul and theirs. His essay on "Spiritual Laws" was, thus, highly characteristic. No American author has so fully exhibited the inseparable relations of style and character. "The student," he says, "is great only by being passive to the superincumbent spirit." His biographers speak of him as "a spiritual-looking boy." He takes exception to the great German, Göethe, by reason of the absence of this higher quality of soul. "I dare not say," he writes, "that Göethe ascended to the highest grounds from which genius has spoken. He is incapable of a self-surrender to the moral sentiment. He can never be dear to men." This deep Emersonian temper amounts, not infrequently, to spiritual passion—what we have called ethical energy of nature, suffusing his being and his authorship. "The word impassioned," says Dr. Holmes, "would seem misplaced, if applied to any of Mr. Emerson's orations." Later on, however, when Emerson had reached the maturity of his powers, the same biographer calls our attention to his "paragraphs glowing with heat."

In fine, his nature was ethical. As Mr. Taine would express it, he was "pre-inclined" to the moral and spiritual. His very culture was of this higher type, the bright exponent of his character and inner life. He could not agree with Mr. Arnold, that culture was purely literary; nor with Mr. Huxley, that it was scientific and philosophic, but rose, without effort, to the high position assumed by Principal Shairp, that it was, first and last, an ethical quality. He speaks, therefore, sympathetically, of the "intellectual conscience"; of the "piety of learning"; of "the unity of thought and morals." "All the chief orators of the world," he says, "have been grave men. Eloquence is the best speech of the best soul." His profound sense of responsibility, as a teacher of men and an author, was one of the expressions of this innate temper of mind. "All writing," he says, "comes of the grace of God," and, when he speaks to us of "the great majesty of style," he refers to those subtle and unseen relations that exist between what a man is interiorly and what he says and does. The closing quatrain of one of his best poems summarily expresses it, wherein he makes human learning tributary to character, as he says—

> "I laugh at the love and the pride of man,
> At the sophist schools and the learned clan,
> For what are they all, in their high conceit,
> When man in the bush with God may meet?"

Turning, for a moment, from praise to adverse criticism, we notice, here, an ethical defect of style, as we noticed a defect purely intellectual. We refer to what has been called, and rightly so, mysticism. "Emerson's poetry," writes Dr. Holmes, "is eminently subjective." So, we may add, is the most of his prose—illustrating that introspective order of style which is not only Platonic and idealistic, but, often, perplexing. To this tendency and quality there are, indeed, notable exceptions. If we survey the lists of themes which Emerson discusses, there is one column of topics so objective in purport that we might classify them under what he calls—Social Aims. Such are—"Man," "The Reformer," "The Young American," "Politics," "Land," "Wealth," "Civilization," "Domestic Life," "War," "The Fugitive Slave Law," "Farming," and "The Future of the Republic." What could be more pertinent and freer from the mystical? Even here, however, though the theme be practical, the discussion is psychologic, and, often, visionary. He speaks of his own "tendency to introversion." Carlyle tells him that "he is too ethical and speculative." One of his biographers calls him "an intellectual mystic." He was, thereby, attracted to the Oriental systems of religion, such as Brahmanism, in the study of which he could give full scope to the love of the weird and the partially revealed. He believed in the Over-Soul—the all-embracing Unity. His piety, as his philosophy, was transcendental, super-rational and, at times, apparently contra-rational. He moved under the guidance of the inner light. "I think nothing is of any value in books," he says, "save the transcendental and extraordinary. Therefore all books of the imagination endure."

Under the control of this ethical reverie, it is not strange that his style often becomes nebulous and uncertain, leading us on through a kind of Nirvana to a condition of semi-consciousness, rather than out and aloft into the open air of clearness and life. "His facts are true in themselves," says Matthew Arnold, "if understood in a certain high sense." To that high sense many of his most appreciative readers often fail to come, possibly because the author himself was outside of himself when he penned the facts. Mr. Emerson, despite his paper on "The Over-Soul," was, in no true sense, a Pantheist. His style, however, is, at times, Pantheistic, if we mean by that epithet visionary and mystical. The moral rises to the spiritual, and the spiritual over-reaches itself in the form of romantic reverie.

This defect conceded, however, it is but occasional and partial, and does not materially detract from the high merit of the style of our author, on its ethical side. The point of importance is, that when Mr. Emerson writes, he does so under the guidance of his heart and conscience and, mainly, because he could not do otherwise. His sense of indebtedness to God and man and to the interests of truth was so pronounced and vital, that he took up the pen somewhat as the old prophets took it up, with the "burden of the Word of the Lord" upon him, to which, willingly or unwillingly, his readers must give heed. He was, in the best sense, a conscientious author, and it is of the Bible and the sacred books of the world and such spiritual volumes as "The Imitation of Christ" and "The Thoughts of Pascal" that he significantly says—"that they are for the closet, and to be read on bended knee." If this is Pantheism in thought or style, we must make the most of it.

III. Literary Tone and Spirit. We have spoken of Emerson's face as intellectual and ethical in its expression. It is, also, of the specifically literary type, indicating the author's natural right to a place among what Dr. Holmes calls, the "Academic Races of New England." Observers speak of that "look of refinement" which his countenance wore; that "cheerful intelligent face" which, in his own language, "is the end of culture."

We have spoken in other connections of the favorite themes which Emerson discussed. If we classify them as intellectual, ethical and literary, it is highly suggestive to note that the last predominate, there being no less than thirty different essays upon literary topics. A few representative examples may be cited, such as, "The Man of Letters," "Persian Poetry," "The Progress of Culture," "Books," "Eloquence," "Beauty," "Literature," "Shakespeare," "The Poet," "Göethe, the Writer," "Literary Ethics" and such separate critiques as those of Carlyle and Thoreau; Burns, Scott and Montaigne. His earliest tastes and efforts, at the Boston Latin School and at Harvard, were not only mentally mature, but were so in the literary sense. Students of his writings must have been impressed with the special satisfaction that he seemed to experience when called upon to address academic students on some commanding theme appertaining to English and American Letters, as he so often did at Harvard, Dartmouth and other literary centres.

Equally noticeable is what we may call his literary knowledge—his wide acquaintance with authors and books, ancient and modern; native and foreign. Especially, in his papers on Shakespeare and Literature and Books is this wealth of literary information seen as he goes over, in cursory manner, the leading names in the world's catalogue of writers. He is never weary of calling our attention to his appreciation of literature and literary men. "The best heads that ever existed," he tells us, "were quite too wise to undervalue letters. A great man should be a great reader." He speaks of the "power and joy" that belong to the career of letters; congratulates those who are committed to such a career and bids them God-speed in its prosecution. We question whether, in the entire collection of his essays, there are finer paragraphs and pages than those in which he is aiming to exhibit the special gift and graces of Edward Evcrett as an orator and a master of language. The eulogium occurs in his paper on "Life and Letters in New England," and is so continuously brilliant and suggestive as to make any special quotation invidious.

Moreover, he is ever intent upon magnifying the office of the author as one of marked superiority and worthy of the best efforts of the best men. In his essay on "Göethe, the Writer," he confines himself to this exalted theme, stating that "men are born to write"; that there have been times when the writer "was a sacred person"; "that talent alone cannot make a writer"; that "behind the book there must be a man."

If we inquire, more specifically, as to any separate evidences of literary spirit in Emerson's prose, we note—

I. The Poetic Element. At times, it takes the form of the graphic or picturesque, the pictorial or imaginative. expression of ideas. It is not our purpose to discuss, here, the poetry of Mr. Emerson as a distinctive form of literary art. It is in point, however, to affirm, that the best function fulfilled by his poetry is seen in the effect that it had upon the tone and spirit of his prose. It gave to his prose that poetic flavor that so much of it possesses, so that it is not aside from truth to say, that Mr. Emerson's best appearance as a poet, is in his prose, and not in his verse. Hence, the frequent recurrence, especially in his literary essays, of passages of marked poetic beauty, as in the following, "The Gothic cathedral is a Missionary in stone"; "Character is like an acrostic—read it forward, backward or across, it still spells the same thing"; "When a man lives with God, his voice shall be as sweet as the murmur of the brook and the rustle of the corn," and, so, on. Some of the most satisfactory essays he has written are those which deal with Beauty, as a faculty and sensibility; as mental, moral and æsthetic in its type; as defying definition, and, yet, as everywhere present and primarily essential to human happiness. He calls it "the pilot of the young soul"; "the form under which the intellect prefers to study the world," and exalts the person and charms of womanhood, in that beauty, as a quality, is presumptively identified therewith.

Not infrequently, this poetic element is the direct expression of a high order of imaginative power,—of that "vision and faculty divine" whose exercise is by no means confined to the one department of verse. He calls the imagination "the precursor of the reason"; "the cardinal human power"; the source of the religions and literatures of the world; the explanation of all true eloquence; the corrective of all lower and sensual tendency.

If we make the distinction between the philosophic and the poetic imagination, the prose of Emerson evinces the presence of each, and in such unity of effect that it would be impossible and undesirable to disjoin them. As we have seen, his philosophy itself was Platonic, and, therefore, poetic, while his poetry, in turn, should we study it, would be found to be philosophic. We are speaking, however, of imagination in the literary sense, and too little emphasis, as we believe, has been placed upon it as manifested in the writings before us. He loved the Oriental mind largely because of its imaginative type. He loved to look an abstract truth in the eye until it became more and more palpable and concrete. His paragraphs evince an ever stronger effort to peer into the unseen; to tread paths hitherto untrodden; to soar with Milton into the highest heaven or, with Dante, to descend to the lowest hell, if so be truths unknown to the logical understanding and unprovable by logical process, might be seen in their own light, and put to silence all misgiving. Hence it is that it is not difficult to find in these essays passages of undoubted sublimity, as in the papers on Plato and Swedenborg, Shakespeare and Göethe; as in the discussion of some abstract theme, such as, "Heroism" or "History." The cast of his character was majestic. The order of his mind was majestic. It was morally impossible for him to descend from the high plane of his thought and life to any lower levels, so that when he came to the act of written expression, he must present "high thinking" in high forms, and illustrate in every line and page that elevation of spirit and sentiment on which Longinus so insists.

2. If Dignity of style is essentially literary, Emerson furnished it above measure. It was a family trait, as seen so conspicuously in his brother Charles. It was a personal and constitutional bias of mind. His demeanor was marked by a kind of classical decorum—by that lofty "urbanity" of presence and bearing which subdued all that was unrefined and gave a courtly character to the place and hour. That immoderateness of speech and statement which in his paper on "The Superlative,' he so justly condemns, was especially revolting to him, in that it was so out of keeping with that lofty and dispassionate reserve which is one of the marks of a man of letters and makes him a guide to his fellows. Hyperbole, he would argue, was unliterary because undignified. Judicious authors never italicize.

3. In perfect consistency with this classical reserve, we often find in Emerson's prose a good degree of Personal Pleasantry—a kind of literary *abandon*, as he would call it, quite essential to the fullest utterance of the truth and of the personality of the writer. In this respect, the style of Emerson is flexible and vivacious; never commonplace and trivial, though often conversational and entertaining. In some of his most erudite and elaborate papers, while he has never descended, he has often condescended, and we see the man, the teacher

and the friend, as well as the philosopher. His paper on "The Superlative" is replete with this humorous banter, not unmixed with satire and allusion. He tells young men anxious to understand Carlyle, "that it needs something more than a clean shirt and reading German to visit him"; "Chemistry," he says, "has taught us that we eat gas, drink gas, tread on gas and *are* gas." He contrasts the homely speech of the village blacksmith or the farmer with the involved periods of the public functionary who "would speak the whole English language three times over" in one speech. "The clergyman who would live in the city," he writes, "*may* have piety, but *must* have taste." In his essays on Thoreau and the Brook-Farm experiment, he misses no opportunity of exposing visionary schemes and holding his readers to plain New England sense.

We prize this open-handed, colloquial manner of Emerson all the more because it is unexpected, and we meet a manly, unconventional, practical author where we expected to meet a scholar and recluse.

These literary qualities conceded, however, we are confronted, at once, by the critics, who are slow to attribute to Emerson's prose any high degree of literary excellence. We are told by Mr. Arnold, as their mouthpiece, that he is not to be placed "among the great writers or the great men of letters"; that his prose has not "the requisite wholeness of good tissue"; that it is not "by a kind of native necessity, true and sound"—

in a word, "that he has not a genius and an instinct for style." This criticism is, partly, true and, partly, misleading. In speaking of the literary character of Emerson's prose, we have purposely used the words, tone and spirit, and have insisted that the prose is pervaded by literary principles; that its tendency or drift is literary; that there is a something in it and about it that must be called by this name; that it is the product of a man and a mind conversant with truth in its literary features and with men of letters as a class; that in theme, discussion and motive, there is the presence of taste, beauty imagination, poetic appreciation, culture. All this is true.

If, however, we extend the word literary as applied, and rightly applied, to the *outer form* of the prose—to its visible dress and texture, Mr. Arnold and the critics are mainly right. Mr. Emerson's prose is literary in tone. In technique, it is not. There is a lack of verbal and structural finish, as seen, for example, in Mr. Arnold's prose or in that of Mr. Lowell. Dr. Holmes is thus obliged to speak of his "archaisms and unusual phrases"; of his "semi-detached sentences." We are told "that his grammar is often embarrassed," while the author himself is frank enough to speak of his "impassable paragraphs, each sentence an infinitely repellant particle." There is such a thing as a sense of form—a keen and delicate appreciation of fitness in word and sentence.

If we may be allowed so to express it, Emerson's

prose is æsthetic, but not artistic. It evinces taste and beauty, though these are not always embodied in the most appropriate external dress. In the sense in which De Quincey and Macaulay and Addison are literary, he is not, and it is this that Mr. Arnold must mean when he says that he had not "an instinct for style"—that he was not an artist in the domain of letters. If Mr. Arnold means more than this, we must demur to his critical judgment. Though not literary in one sense, in another and an equally significant sense, Mr. Emerson is so.

Literature, we insist, is more than word and phrase. It is these, with the thought and the thinker behind them. Style is more than outer form and finish. It is these, with the inner form beneath them. A writer and a man of letters is more than a verbal artist. He is an exponent of mind and heart, conscience and taste, and expresses on the page, in vital manner, the deepest impulses of his soul.

Emerson's prose is open to criticism at the hands of the technical critic, as failing, at times, to present the thought in faultless verbal dress. To this extent he is unliterary, but not beyond this, and when we say that he wrote literary English Prose as Bacon and Milton wrote it; as Coleridge and Carlyle and Thomas Arnold wrote it, we give him a place, and a rightful place, among "great writers and great men of letters."

It remains, therefore, to inquire as to—His True

Position in American Literature and Life. It is clear that Mr. Emerson cannot be justly called a popular writer, as Macaulay and Lamb, Irving and Lowell are popular. The type of his mind and art is too intellectual and ethical to admit of it. His circle of readers and admirers will always be limited, constituting what may be termed—a cult or an order—as represented by the Concord School, with its defined adherents. In his paper on "Spiritual Laws," when speaking of literary patronage and reputation, he remarks, "Only those books come down which deserve to last. There are not in the world, at any one time, more than a dozen persons who read and understand Plato, yet to every generation those come duly down, for the sake of these few, as if God brought them in his hand." Mr. Emerson himself did not anticipate general patronage. He was wise enough to know the fact and the reason of his own literary limitations, and is now receiving, at the hands of the modern public, just what he expected to receive—"fit audience, though few." As Mr. Arnold states it, "He is the friend and aider of those who live in the spirit."

If we inquire definitely as to his mission and ministry among us, we answer that it was in the high direction of mental stimulus and ethical ennobling.

> "His was the task, and his the lordly gift,
> Our eyes, our hearts bent earthward, to uplift."

Among what he calls "The Uses of Great Men," no use could be grander, and no one has more devotedly and successfully fulfilled it. There is a sense, indeed, in which Emerson's personal and literary influence may be said to be unlimited, in that it has so entered into the structure and higher habit of modern American life as to have become a substantive part of it, incapable of separation. As Dr. Holmes suggests, this is a far more important fact and far more to the permanent renown of any author, than that he should have written a poem or an essay or a series of essays, widely current and popular. Better by far to have impressed himself as an author indelibly upon the mind and heart of a generation and for all time than to have done this or that in the line of specific literary work. Modern English and American Literature will never lose its Emersonian impression, and when we say that, we say something that designates, as nothing else can, the intrinsic excellence of our author's work. Not only did he impress men, here and there, as he did Carlyle and Coleridge, Channing and Lowell, but he stamped the seal of his personality as a man and a writer upon his age and nation so as to give them new direction and impulse. His influence, as has been said, is not only visible on the surface of our thought, but "ploughed into it." One of the distinguishing marks of his genius is seen in the fact that he had more influence on his age than his age had on him, and Matthew Arnold, with highest eulogium, classes him with Wordsworth, as he says—"that these two, respectively, have done the most important work in English prose and poetry in the present century." From no two volumes of English prose can a larger number of significant passages be gathered, and who could estimate the stimulating effect of the presence of a few such supreme intellects in any institution or age or nation. As he remarked of his personal friend, Dr. Channing, "that all America would have been impoverished in wanting him," so can we say of Emerson. He is the "common property" of the intellectual public, and we could not spare him from our corporate literary life any more than we could spare Bacon and Milton and Dr. Johnson. In his essay on "Books," he tells us that he finds certain books "vital and spermatic." Emerson's books, we may add, are "vital and spermatic," full of life and full of seminal virtue, and must be read by every man who is truly ambitious to reach the highest mental and ethical ends. Is it too much to say, that the appreciative perusal of Emerson is an education and an inspiration, quickening into new activity, what he calls, in speaking of Milton—"the vibration of hope, self-reverence, piety and beauty!" For such a reading there is a kind of preparative work that is essential—a clearing of the inner eye; a cleaning of the conscience, mind and sentiment, if so be, that through the medium of fullest affinity, the author and the reader may understand each other, and the giving and receiving be complete.

We emphasize, as a final word, the urgent need of this Emersonian Element in Modern Life and Letters; partly, by reason of its inherent value and, partly, to rebuke the ever-increasing tendency to the unintellectual and unethical in literature and style. Of this debasing tendency, the author was himself aware, as he asks with imploring pathos—"Amidst the downward proneness of things, will you not tolerate one or two solitary voices in the land, speaking for thoughts and principles not marketable or perishable?" "If our times are sterile in genius, we must cheer us with books of believing men who had atmosphere and amplitude about them." "It is a sort of mark of probity to declare how little you believe, and we have punctuality for faith and good taste for character." "How is the new generation to be edified?" he asks, and as quickly answers with eloquent earnestness—by bringing in a new and sublime order of men, who "with happy hearts and a bias for theism bring duty and magnanimity once again into vogue." This is Emerson and this is Emersonianism—pure and simple, ethical and mental and literary, and of no type of character and culture is the present age and nation more in need. Despite defects of logical method, ethical consistency and verbal finish—this is the style, after all, and this the literature for which the world is waiting. What we need, most of all, in authorship is personality behind it and character behind it and the highest purposes inspiring it. What we seek in books, first and last, is stimulus and uplifting, even though, at times, such high result be reached at the possible expense of executive form and finish. Literature is embodied intellect and character in verbal form. It is power in possession and power in exercise, and when we read an author we are to feel, as we do feel in reading Emerson, that literature is richer than ever for such books ; that human character is richer than ever for such men ; that truth is safer than ever with such defenders and that life is a happier and holier thing in that "Such as these have lived and died," and live again and shall never die.

EMERSON'S STYLE.

Examples.

Among secular books, Plato only is entitled to Omar's fanatical compliment to the koran, when he said—"Burn the libraries; for their value is in this book." These sentences contain the culture of nations; these are the corner-stone of schools; these are the fountain-head of literatures. . . . . There was never such range of speculation. Out of Plato came all things that are still written and debated among men of thought. Great havoc makes he among our originalities. —"*Representative Men.*"

It is contended by those who have been bred at Eton, Harrow, Rugby and Westminster, that the public sentiment within each of these schools is heightened and manly; that in their playgrounds, courage is universally admired; meanness, despised; manly feelings and generous conduct are encouraged; that an unwritten code of honor deals to the spoiled child of rank and to the child of upstart wealth an even-handed justice, purges their nonsense out of both and does all that can be done to make them gentlemen. Again, at the universities, it is urged that all goes to form, what England values as the flower of its national life—a well-educated gentleman.—"*English Traits.*"

There is not yet any inventory of a man's faculties, any more than a bible of his opinions. Who shall set a limit to the influence of a human being? There are men who by their sympathetic attractions carry nations with them and lead the activity of the human race. And if there be such a tie, that wherever the mind of man goes, nature will accompany him, perhaps there are men whose magnetisms are of that force to draw material and elemental powers, and where they appear, immense instrumentalities organize around them. Life is a search after power; and this is an element with which the world is so saturated that no honest seeking goes unrewarded.—"*Conduct of Life.*"

I like to be beholden to the great metropolitan English speech, the sea which receives tributaries from every region under heaven. I should as soon think of swimming across Charles River when I wish to go to Boston, as of reading my books in originals when I have them rendered for me in my mother-tongue.—"*Society and Solitude.*"

CONCLUDING CHAPTER.

INDEPENDENT LITERARY JUDGMENTS.

WITHIN the sphere of general intellectual life, thought or thinking may be said to be conditioned in its freedom by certain well-understood limitations.

What we term, *unwritten precedent* or *tradition*, is one of these conditions, gathering volume and authority as the generations pass, until, at length it may be said to have all the force of definitely expressed and carefully recorded truth. With the great body of the people, as distinct from the specially educated classes, such antecedent oral testimony is practically final in its sanctions, while, with the enlightened classes themselves, it enters as an important factor in the reaching of conclusions. Conspicuously influential in many branches of the church as bearing on questions of faith and order, its influence is more or less apparent in every province of intellectual life and among all classes of minds. With not a few, indeed, traditional teachings may be said to be the only form of authority on which they rely.

In addition to such a limitation, there is what is included in the *history* of *opinion*, the *consensus gentium*, the gathered testimony of all peoples and all ages, in so far as it bears on those particular phases of mental inquiry that from time to time engage us as thinkers. As far as it goes, we possess in this a valid and helpful limitation of individual belief, far in advance of any form of mere traditional authority. It is the written and matured view of all those who have done the most and the best thinking. Such a consensus has the great advantage of representing a vast variety of judgment, and covers in its area of observation all countries and centuries. It is public opinion expanded in its range to the extent of universality. Presumably, therefore, it is a wise and well-digested body of opinion, the carefully generalized result of ages of reflection. If this be so, our general mental judgments will be controlled by such an aggregate of testimony, just in proportion to its age, its compass and the opportunity afforded for its true expression.

Other conditions, still, are seen to enter as affecting our common intellectual life, such as—personal *prejudice*, personal *pride* and selfish interest. The very *environment* in the midst of which our life has been placed and the particular type of training, in the home and the school, to which we have been subjected, give coloring and character to our beliefs. The wish is, often, the father of the thought. We, often, think in this or that direction through the sheer force of inherited habit, or by a kind of unconscious imitation of the methods of others more independent than we are. In fact, we think so much along the lines of precedent and accumulated opinion and personal bias and surroundings, that it is difficult, if not impossible, for us to draw the boundary between our thinking, as thus circumscribed, and as indeed our own, the veritable expression of our own mental insight and outlook. All such conditions have their appropriate place in the province of thought, and are so essential as checks and barriers to unlimited speculation, that, without their restrictive influence, liberty of opinion might degenerate into the wildest license.

All this conceded, however, there is such a thing as independent intellectual judgment, quite apart from all precedent, historical beliefs, prejudice and environment, an order of judgment binding, to some good degree, on every man who is entitled to the name of thinker, and absolutely essential to any such thing as personal mental progress. Be the limitations of thought what they may, unless scholars and students rise above them and pass beyond them, out into the open area of free inquiry and discussion, what Bacon calls, the advancement of learning, will be rendered impossible.

Precisely so is it in the narrower sphere of literature and style. Here, also, individual judgment is, in a sense, dependent, and rightly so. It is affected by literary precedent, unwritten and intangible though it be; affected, still more perceptibly, by that great volume of concurrent testimony known as literary history; affected, still further, and, most especially, by the expressed conclusions of literary ctiticism, and, still again, by environment, education, personal preferences and personal interests. All these restrictions are, in a measure, legitimate in the realm of letters, and, whether we desire it or not, will assert their presence and shape our deductions. In their proper place and function, they are to be accepted by us as being what Coleridge would call, aids to reflection, making it easier for us to think, and making it less difficult for us to break over the barriers established by historic usage.

Here, again, however, as in the wider mental area, there must be a limit to limitation itself. With the open volume of the past before us, we must be allowed to attempt, at least, to reach some literary conclusions of our own. With all proper deference to those who have preceded us, we are not bound to swear in the words of any master. We are, rather, bound, in behalf of literary interests, to do our own thinking in our own way, and having secured conclusions of our own sanctioned by our best reason and study, to hold thereto with tenacity and courage.

A more definite inquiry as to the Condition and the Need of such independence of view in matters of literature is now in place.

I. Private judgment in Style and Letters is based, first of all, on Literary Study and Scholarship. The mere tyro or amateur in this department has no more right to pronounce his opinion as a final one, than has any superfical observer in any branch of learning a right to insist that his half-digested conclusions shall be accepted by others. Here, as everywhere else, liberty of view involves a measure of responsibility. In fact, the wider the freedom, the greater is the duty of painstaking procedure, lest what is meant to conserve, in the end, the highest literary interests, shall be seen to impair and possibly nullify them. The free-thinker, in the best sense, is he who looks upon his liberty in the light of a high privilege and trust, for which he is to be held accountable, and not at all as a warrant to ignore all rational procedure.

By literary study as a basis of judgment we mean, a thorough examination of the special subject or class of subjects before the student at the time. This involves something more than a hasty glance, such as would seem to have sufficed many so-called literary critics. It involves an inspection of the subject in all its connections, bearings and possible applications. In literature, as elsewhere, one truth involves the notice of all related truths, that comparative order of research which, in its compass and minuteness, loses sight of no fact or principle that may contribute light to the main discussion.

Such a study will necessarily include a careful

survey of the history of literary opinion on the special topic under treatment. The literary student must, at this point, be the literary historian, thoroughly conversant with all that has been written pertinent to the question. He must, as we say, cover the ground; look at literature as but one of the endlessly diversified departments of human thought; carefully noting how it affects them and how it is affected by them, and be able to trace the course of the subject in hand from its entrance into literature, on through the successive stages of its expression to its present status. General knowledge, of whatever kind, will not do here. It must be literary and special, so that the critic will not be guilty of the error so often committed, of broaching an opinion as original when it has existed, perhaps, for a series of years, in the literary records of the nation. As the ambitious inventor, with his scientific instrument or theory in hand, must be well aware, before he offers it as new, that the Patent Office officials have not long since received and filed its prototype, so must the student of questions in authorship be on his guard lest he be grossly ignorant of those who have anticipated his so-called independent inferences. Such judgments are independent to a fault, ignorantly or recklessly regardless of antecedent opinion, and earning a temporary credit for insight, at the expense of history and their own subsequent repute. English and American literary criticism is full of this unseemly error; and all the more confirms the urgent need of thorough scholarship as a warrant for free opinion and a guarantee that opinion, in so far as it departs from historical judgment, is deserving of thoughtful attention. It is he, and he only, who, after due examination of what others have said, still insists on being heard, that fully deserves to be heard, and, in all probability, has arrived at results substantially his own.

II. We mark a further condition of private judgment in letters in—The ability to give Satisfactory Reasons for such judgment. The conservative attitude of the great majority of men demands such reasons, and, in the nature of the case, they are rightly demanded. He who advances a new view has the presumption against him and the burden of proof upon him. He must satisfy every doubtful mind that what he advances is not a mere hypothesis, unsupported by history or logic, but a rational result in the domain of letters, reached by rational methods and justifying its presence as a new view, among all accepted theories and beliefs.

It is possible that, here and there in the course of history, a literary student or critic may be found whose decisions are intuitive rather than inductive, and who knows what he knows despite all inability to explain it. It might, moreover, be true that, where no such genius exists, the average literary scholar might reach results in advance of all "existing" opinion, and, yet, be unable satisfactorily to explain the grounds and methods of his work.

This, however, is exceptional. Inventors must explain their inventions, if, indeed, they wish to have them accepted and currently used. Advocates of new theories in any department, must present their credentials and invite acceptance by confirmatory evidence. In one sense, any man may think for himself as freely and as loosely as he pleases, and may follow his speculations whithersoever they may conduct him. When, however, he comes to us with his ascertained judgments, for our endorsement, looseness must give place to logic, and we must insist upon proof, positive and sufficient. It is well that it is so, or the world of letters would be over-run with the most unfounded fancies, and literature itself become the butt of satirists and comedians.

If it is insisted, as it is, that the alleged Baconian authorship of the Shakespearean plays is a tenable one; that the majority of the best English authors are of Celtic rather than Teutonic ancestry; that such a poet as Whitman is a bard of the first literary order; that Mr. Wilde's æsthetic view of literature is correct; that Wordsworth's present popularity is undeserved, and that prevailing journalistic criticism is, in the main, reliable—then must we understand clearly the reasons for such radical opinions, and be able to weigh them over against all accepted views on these respective topics. Such reasons being adduced, we are not only warranted in accepting them, but are bound to accept them. Independent judgment is, in this sense, dependent, that it must proceed, judicially and dispassionately, to its conclusions, but so proceeding, it is made imperative upon every intelligent reader to give it credence.

III. Scarcely less important as a condition of such freedom, is An Unbiased Mind, marked by that candor and conscientiousness so germane to the truly critical spirit and so essential to all beneficent result. We touch, at this point, what is, perhaps, the most difficult of all conditions to meet. Keeping in due abeyance the personal element on its objectionable side, while, at the same time, exalting personal opinion to the position which it rightly claims, is no easy matter to compass. In reaching conclusions which are characteristically our own, and, as such, personal, special care must be taken lest this personal element overreach itself and defeat the very purpose in view. How difficult, here, to annul the ever-intruding influence of pride of opinion as to questions of authorship! In what various and insidious forms will our own prejudices seek to enter and modify our reasoning! What a potent influence passion and selfish interest may exert to thwart the natural operation of the truth! How, as suggested, our peculiar training or environment may unduly bias our judgment, and we be really the least ourselves when we think we are the most so! The history of criticism, at this point, would make another volume of what Mr. Disraeli has named,

"The Curiosities of Literature,"—a large proportion of such a review of books and authors being utterly misleading by reason of the presence of these personal elements on the baser side.

In this respect, such critical historians as Gibbon and Buckle grievously erred, in passing the limit of independence properly assigned them. It was when Bacon was insisting on sincerity in matters of literary opinion, that he wrote his dedication of "The Advancement of Learning," to James I., in which he fairly gets down on all fours, in the most slavish adulation, as he says—"There has not been since Christ's time, any king so learned in all literature, divine and human," to which he adds, with even greater emphasis. "This is no amplification, at all, but a positive and measured truth." So low can a man's better nature bow, without shame, to his baser.

IV. We note, as a final condition,—The spirit of Modest Reserve. Independent as our decisions may be and ought to be, they are to be stated with a due regard to the conflicting opinions of others equally thoughtful, and with a deep conviction of our liability to err. The very principle of private judgment for which we contend, demands some concession to those who claim a similar liberty; no man in literature, or anywhere else, can afford to regard himself as final authority. The Autocrats of Literature are far too numerous, nor is high-headed dogmatism confined to theology and morals. Sincere devotion to the interests of truth will make it necessary for any man, however wise, to speak with some reserve; to become modestly suspicious, at times, of his own wisdom; to recall what he has perchance looked upon as settled, and to think more of truth than of himself. Great critics, as a rule, have been marked by modesty. The names of Longinus and Lessing and Sainte-Beuve, and even Göethe, will suffice to confirm this statement, while it especially becomes all lesser names in literary art, to possess the grace of humility, and say what they say with courage, and, yet, subject to possible revision or withdrawal. The Pope at Rome is the only man who claims to be infallible, and, for that very reason, is not so.

Such are the requisites of freedom of judgment in literature which, being met, furnish a valid claim to such freedom. Every student and critic of authority is, in every good sense, a free man and a free thinker, insisting on his right in this regard, and, next to the possession of the truth itself, prizing nothing more highly than the unrestricted search after it and expression of it by voice and pen.

We are now prepared to note the Need and Duty of such Literary Independence.

I. It may be said to be a duty lying in the line of Self-Respect. Every student of letters owes it to himself, after duly regarding the opinions of others, to reach and defend his own conclusions.

Any other course would beget within him the worst form of mental dependence and a slavish deference to tradition. Better to err on the side of an undue reliance upon individual research and reflection in matters of style and criticism, than on the side of an unthinking acceptance of existing theories and beliefs. Better the bold procedure of Mr. Gosse, in his unique adulation of the inferior poets prior to Pope, than the time-serving spirit of those who are ambitious to reproduce the *dicta* of their more distinguished forerunners. Such a critic as Carlyle has his conspicuous faults of prejudice and one-sidedness, and, yet, no man can afford to be ignorant of his conclusions or to decry them, and, that, mainly, for the reason that they are, from first to last, *his* conclusions, characteristic of his genius and germane to his own way of thinking. Unique in their conception and expression, they take their place among the few original deliverances in literature. Doctor Samuel Johnson possessed this independent spirit, and in his "Lives of the English Poets," conspicuously evinced it. Mr. Arnold, of England, and Mr. Emerson, of America, their errors conceded, have retained their self-respect as critics by an unswerving adherence to what they deemed to be true. The same is true of the late Mr. Whipple, a man who, in justice to himself, did his own thinking, and, for this reason, among others, advanced the art of literary criticism in America to a level of dignity and value not hitherto reached. Mr. Stedman, in poetry, and Mr. Lowell, in general literature, have modestly illustrated the same unshackled freedom of judgment.

II. The need of such liberty is especially seen in —the Number and Importance of Unsettled Questions in Literature and Style. This area of open questions is ever widening with the general widening of thought, and such questions must, in the nature of the case, be apprehended, discussed, and decided in an untrammelled manner, with large catholicity of outlook and a sincere desire to reach the truth, be its agreement with truth already reached manifest or not. We may examine, for a moment, a few of these open inquiries which force themselves, in such an era as this, upon every intelligent student of literary product, and demand of him an examination of them which shall be fully his own. What is the meaning of literature itself, and what is its definite province as distinct from all related provinces; what is the place of the ethical element in authorship, and is the attitude of Principal Shairp and of Selkirk regarding it correct; what is the relation, in the best poetry, of the intellectual element to the impassioned; how are the literary periods of such a nation as the English to be classified, and is the historic classification admissible; what, after all, are the guiding principles of style; what rank should be assigned to fiction as an order of literature, and is Sidney Lanier's view, as represented in his "English Novel," tenable; where is poetry itself to be ranked as a species of literary art, and is not miscellaneous prose underestimated in its nature and value? More specifically still, what place in poetry shall be given to Dryden and Thomson, Keats and Gray, Shelley and Southey; is Dickens, or Thackeray, the first name in English descriptive fiction, and where are we to rank Charlotte Brontë and Hawthorne; what is the status, in English prose, of such authors as, Coleridge and Carlyle, Macaulay and Emerson; what are the comparative merits of such critics as Arnold and Lowell, and Whipple, and where, in truth, are we to place such English poets as Robert Browning, Swinburne and Morris, and is the Laureate himself rightly styled a bard of the first order? These and scores of similar inquiries are, at present, mooted questions in the open parliament of English Letters.

To accept or reject this or that view respecting them only because it comes to us sanctioned by names in high repute, is at once to surrender all claim to literary personality, and to impair the best interests of criticism itself. "To thine own self be true," is the Shakespearean behest, and is here in place. "Be thyself, and no other one," Carlyle would say to us, and we are to give heed to his voice. Want of courage, at this point, to prosecute our researches and abide by our judgments as candidly reached, is itself the best evidence of unfitness for literary work and a suficient summons to betake ourselves to other and less responsible spheres, where but one man in a hundred or a thousand is expected to think, and all the others are to follow his leading. Intellectual and literary processes somewhat change from age to age. Standards themselves are varied, and under the pressure of the increasing complexity of life and thought, yield to other criteria. The ideas and ideals of one age or people will not necessarily or presumably do for another. Writers of the first rank in the sixteenth century, may justly be consigned to second and third positions, in the nineteenth, as those in turn who were their inferiors may be accorded a higher place. Because Shakespeare was not appreciated in the time of Elizabeth, and is not even mentioned by Doctor Johnson, in his "Lives of the Poets," we cannot justly argue for his neglect in our day. Wordsworth, the target of all the criticism of his time, may possibly deserve the ever-increasing interest now exhibited in his work, while such authors as Denham, Davenant, Cowley and Waller, despite all contemporary praise, must in justice be required to make room for worthier bards and writers.

In fine, literary progress demands literary independence, as mental progress demands mental independence, or as progress in any science or art demands therein a legitimate freedom of view. To tell us that Spenser's "Faerie Queen," is equally able or attractive throughout its entire development, is to tell us what others possibly believe, but what we do not and cannot believe until better evidence is forthcoming than has as yet been adduced.

The same remark is true of Milton's longest epic. To say that Shakespeare is so correct a verbal artist that no change of line or word, in play or sonnet, can be safely made, is not only in violation of the doctrine of human fallibility, but counter to the facts of verbal criticism and the radical law of change in language. To place such a poet as Thomas Gray as high as some recent writers have placed him, obliges us indeed to examine carefully the grounds of our dissent, but by no means is it necessary to withdraw our dissent. To endorse, in any valid sense, much of the tenor of modern opinion as to the poetic merit of the school of Whitman, is altogether impossible, though the oracle at Delphi order it. To tell us that the dramatic poetry of Robert Browning is, as a whole, intelligible to any reader of average ability, does not compel us either to avow that it is thus intelligible to us, or to take our place, thereby, below the level of the average mind. Our own literary progress and that of literature itself, is dependent on our having literary opinions of our own, based on sufficient reasons ready at demand and, as such, tenaciously held, until by, a similar exercise of freedom of thought, we see the way clear to a change of view.

Tradition, the history of opinion, and other elements, perchance, are partial factors in reaching safe results in criticism, but the most essential of all is personal reflection and study. With the life and times of authors before us, and their published works actually in hand, there is no good reason why every student of fair ability should not examine and decide for himself. In no republic is freedom of thought so essential as in that of letters. In no one is there greater need of a declaration of independence against all intellectual tyranny. That intellectual development of Europe of which Dr. Draper has so brilliantly written, is mainly the result of the emancipation of modern thought, and that Literary Development of England and America, now in process, and yet to assume more imposing forms, is to be the normal outgrowth of that personality of opinion which always keeps in view the clearly marked course of historic criticism, and also remembers that there are times when it must courteously and courageously depart therefrom. The spirit of mental and literary servility is by no means dead, and, in this unthinking age, often threatens to crush out all that is noblest and best. Under safe limitations, logical and ethical, the right and duty of private judgment in style and literature are to be as fully emphasized as Milton emphasized them within the sphere of English Politics.

INDEX.

INDEX.